THE PRINCIPAL AS

Early Literacy Leader

Introduction to the *Leading Student Achievement* Series

The *Leading Student Achievement* series is a joint publication of the Ontario Principals' Council (OPC) and Corwin Press as part of an active commitment to support and develop excellent school leadership. One of the roles of OPC is to identify, design, develop, and deliver workshops that meet the learning needs of school leaders. Most of the handbooks in this series were originally developed as one-day workshops by their authors to share their expertise in key areas of school leadership. The five handbooks in this series are these:

The Principal as Professional Learning Community Leader

The Principal as Data-Driven Leader

The Principal as Early Literacy Leader

The Principal as Instructional Leader in Literacy

The Principal as Mathematics Leader

Each handbook in the *Leading Student Achievement* series is grounded in action and is designed as a hands-on, practical guide to support school leaders in their roles as instructional leaders. From novice principals who are assuming the principalship to experienced principals who are committed to continuous learning, readers from all levels of experience will benefit from the accessible blend of theory and practice presented in these handbooks. The provision of practical strategies that principals can use immediately in their schools makes this series a valuable resource to all who are committed to improving student achievement.

THE PRINCIPAL AS

Early Literacy Leader

LEADING STUDENT ACHIEVEMENT
SERIES

A Joint Publication

ONTARIO
PRINCIPALS'
COUNCIL
Exemplary Leadership
in Public Education

For information:

Corwin Press
A SAGE Company
2455 Teller Road
Thousand Oaks, California 91320
www.corwinpress.com

SAGE Ltd.
1 Oliver's Yard
55 City Road
London EC1Y 1SP
United Kingdom

SAGE India Pvt. Ltd.
B 1/I 1 Mohan Cooperative
Industrial Area
Mathura Road, New Delhi 110 044
India

SAGE Asia-Pacific Pte. Ltd.
33 Pekin Street #02-01
Far East Square
Singapore 048763

Printed in the United States of America.

Library of Congress Cataloging-in-Publication Data

The principal as early literacy leader/Ontario Principals' Council.
     p. cm.
"A Joint Publication With Ontario Principals' Council."
Includes bibliographical references.
ISBN 978-1-4129-6306-0 (cloth)
ISBN 978-1-4129-6307-7 (pbk.)
     1. Language arts (Early childhood) 2. Literacy programs—Planning.
3. School principals. I. Ontario Principals' Council. II. Title.

LB1139.5.L35P75 2009
372.6—dc22   2008035244

This book is printed on acid-free paper.

08   09   10   11   12   10   9   8   7   6   5   4   3   2   1

Acquisitions Editor:	Debra Stollenwerk
Editorial Assistant:	Allison Scott
Production Editor:	Libby Larson
Copy Editor:	Claire Larson
Typesetter:	C&M Digitals (P) Ltd.
Proofreader:	Theresa Kay
Indexer:	Terri Corry
Cover Designer:	Lisa Riley

Contents

Acknowledgments

The Ontario Principals' Council gratefully acknowledges Sharon Speir, author of *The Principal as Early Literacy Leader.*

Dr. Sharon Speir has a PhD in curriculum teaching and learning from the Ontario Institute for Studies in Education/ University of Toronto, Ontario, Canada. She has demonstrated international, provincial, district, and school leadership as a teacher, consultant, principal, superintendent, and researcher. Her research interests include children's thinking, teacher theories, school-based research, and qualitative designs. She is currently a superintendent of schools with the Rainbow District School Board, where she has responsibility for managing information for student achievement. She has taught the principal qualifications programs and Vital Signs: Taking the Pulse of Your School (Data-Based Decision Making) workshops for the Ontario Principals' Council. Her background in the early years and early literacy includes an undergraduate degree in Child Studies from the University of Guelph, as well as experience as an administrator of preschool programs and an early years teacher.

As well, the efforts of Ethne Cullen and Linda Massey in coordinating this joint OPC/Corwin project are gratefully acknowledged.

Corwin Press gratefully acknowledges the contributions of the following reviewers:

Emme Barnes
Literacy Facilitator
Hawk Ridge Elementary School
Charlotte, NC

Rochelle Dail, PhD
Assistant Professor
The University of Alabama
Tuscaloosa, AL

Cathy Patterson
Assistant Principal
Walnut Valley USD
Diamond Bar, CA

Erin A. Rivers
Educator; 9–12
Shawnee Mission North High School
Overland Park, KS

Bess Sullivan Scott, PhD
Principal
McPhee Elementary School
Lincoln, NE

Introduction

THE QUESTION

Have you hesitated outside the door of the classroom of three-, four-, or five-year-olds, unsure as to whether you should enter, even less certain of how to enter into the play and conversation of small children? How many of you have wondered if there was not more we could be doing for children at ages three, four, and five years to further their literacy learning?

If these questions sound familiar, you are not alone. Most school leaders readily admit they know very little about the early years! However, a renewed interest in early literacy has many looking to the early years for solutions to the problem of underachievement in literacy and the means to provide early support to children who will struggle with literacy learning later in the primary grades.

TAKE UP THE CHALLENGE

The challenge for educators interested in acquiring a better understanding of the early years is that at first glance, the world of three-, four-, and five-year-olds appears to be a very simple world, structured around some very simple rules as suggested by Robert Fulghum (2003) in his poem, "All I Really Need to Know I Learned in Kindergarten."

> Most of what I really need to know about how to live, and what to do, and how to be, I learned in Kindergarten . . .
> These are the things I learned: Share everything. Play fair. Don't hit people. Put things back where you found them. Clean up your own mess . . .

And then remember the book about Dick and Jane and the first word you learned, the biggest word of all: *LOOK*. Everything you need to know is in there somewhere—The Golden Rule and love and basic sanitation, ecology and politics and sane living. (Fulghum, 2003, pp. 2–3)

Although Fulghum's poem contains wisdom on how to live life, his version of preschool education and early literacy is outdated and serves as a reminder that the general tendency is to oversimplify the learning that occurs in early years before formal school and minimize the role that adults and the environment play in this critical period of learning. This period of learning is far from simple. As we gain a more precise understanding of how the brain works and how it develops, our understanding of how children learn has advanced, and our philosophies about the teaching and learning of young children have also evolved, influenced by the times in which we live. The same can be said for our understanding of the complexity of literacy learning and what it means to be literate.

OUR EVOLVING UNDERSTANDING OF LITERACY

Only 600 years ago, the average citizen did not think about reading, and children were reared to assist with work. Prior to the 1400s, reading was an activity reserved for scholars, the clergy, and the upper class. With the invention of the printing press and the ability to mass-produce books in the 1500s, the Bible became popular and people became interested in reading for themselves.

During the late 1800s and early 1900s, in a predominately agricultural society, the home played a primary role in the raising and socialization of young children. Kindergartens, where they existed, were compared to a garden and children to the germinating seeds. Friedrich Froebel (1782–1852), the originator of the kindergarten, thought that children carried the seed of self-development, and given the right conditions and opportunity, it was thought that, like plants, children would naturally develop. The rate of literacy rose in the late 1800s with an increase in commerce and jobs that required a functional level of literacy, defined as basic reading and writing. In primary school, children were taught to read using simple texts with limited vocabulary.

By the mid-1900s, during the industrial revolution, women entered the workforce in unprecedented numbers, children were no longer cared for primarily in the home, and programs for young children became well established. Psychologists Jean Piaget (1896–1980), Lawrence Kohlberg (1927–1958), and Erik Erikson (1902–1994) each identified stages and critical periods of learning—for cognitive, moral, and social development, respectively. Educators began to design materials and methods with learning in mind. For those paying attention, these new learning approaches and the results they achieved helped to illustrate the largely untapped learning potential of young children. A wonderful example of this is illustrated by Maria Montessori's (1870–1952) approach to educating the children whom society at that time had deemed uneducable—the disabled and disadvantaged. During this time period, children began to be grouped and instructed by age, and expectations for learning were developed according to different ages and stages. By the 1950s, literacy learning was defined as a certain set of habits and skills that effective readers had mastered. To learn to read implied the reinforcement and practice of these skills. A set of programs emerged for reading that included SRA labs, phonics, language experience charts, and eventually whole language.

Now well into the 21st century and the age of globalization, markets are fiercely competitive, and literacy levels have been statistically linked to a nation's economic viability. The pressure is on for children to perform literacy skills at younger and younger ages. Public education institutions are held accountable for achievement results, and programs are required that respond to the perceived gaps, in particular for children who come to school from disadvantaged circumstances or with limited literacy experiences. Early years interventions programs designed to combat the relationship between childhood poverty and school failure, such as those initiated by the Perry Preschool Project (1962) and Head Start (1970), have claimed both short- and long-term effects. The Perry Preschool Project has documented impressive results that include less delinquency, fewer crimes, and less police contact; higher academic achievement, including higher scores on standardized tests of intellectual ability, higher high school grades, fewer school dropouts, and higher rates of high school graduation; higher median annual earnings; greater economic independence; and fewer pregnancies for women at age 19 (Weikart, Bond, & McNeil, 1978).

The expanded definition of literacy now includes communication in a variety of forms.

> UNESCO's concept of literacy has moved beyond the simple notion of a set of technical skills of reading, writing and calculating to one that encompasses multiple dimensions of these competencies. In acknowledging recent economic, political and social transformations—including globalization and the advancement of information and communication technologies (ICTs)—UNESCO recognizes that there are many practices of literacy embedded in different cultural processes, personal circumstances and collective structures.
>
> Literacy is central to all levels of learning, through all delivery modes. Literacy is an issue that concerns everybody. (United Nations Educational, Scientific and Cultural Organization)

Literacy instruction includes reading and writing in a variety of subject areas, differentiation for learning styles, instruction that scaffolds for learning levels, and the explicit teaching of reading and writing strategies.

THE ROLE EARLY LITERACY EXPERIENCE PLAYS IN THE DEVELOPMENT OF THE BRAIN

Where once we thought our brains developed from our genetic gifts, now we understand brain development to be a function of the interaction between genes and experiences. Previously we thought of the experiences before three years of age as limited and with little consequence for later development; now we recognize the early experiences actually change the structural design of the brain. Now we understand that early interactions do more than create a favorable environment for learning—these interactions impact the very development of the brain. We now know there are prime times for learning different kinds of knowledge and skills and that at three years of age, a child's brain is twice as active as an adult's (Shore, 1997). McCain and Mustard (1999, 2002) maintain that the evidence continues to mount to support these conclusions that early-years' experience influences brain development.

> New evidence from neurobiology, animal studies, epidemio-logical and longitudinal studies of populations, interven-tion studies, and observational studies reaffirms that experience-based brain development in the early years of life, including the in utero period, affects learning, behavior, and physical and mental health throughout life. (McCain & Mustard, 2002, p. 5)

Educational philosopher John Dewey (1859–1952) explained that experience teaches—either positively or negatively. Class differences in language development can be detected in the first years of life, and by twenty-four months, differences in vocabulary can be detected among children from different classes. This period of development has a significant effect on later language develop-ment and is strongly related to the words spoken to the child dur-ing the early period of life. Experiences in the early years, whether as a result of challenging circumstances or poorly designed programs, can be detrimental to development or lead to adverse responses later in life. Programs for young children that are suc-cessful empower children through active learning initiated by the children, empower parents by engaging them as partners, and empower teachers with systematic inservice curriculum training and supportive curriculum supervision (Schweinhart, Barnes, & Weikart, 1993).

LEARNING TO BE LITERATE: SO MUCH MORE THAN LEARNING THE CONVENTIONS OF LANGUAGE

The press down of primary education into the early years, the desire to teach the conventions of language (learning to read and write) at younger ages, and the lack of understanding of how young children learn has created a disturbing trend toward the elimination of activity and play in the early years, a move away from the engagement between mother and child and simple word play, toward more structured lessons, often fashioned by commercial publishing companies, imitating more traditional techniques from earlier times and those we would have once seen in later primary school. Early literacy is so much more than alphabet naming, phonemic awareness, and print recognition.

IT STARTS WITH SCHOOL LEADERS

It is only through a better understanding of how young children learn and how they think that, as school leaders, we can ensure that we are developing and providing programs for children that engage and enrich the youngest minds and ensure their success as lifelong learners. This understanding is important for the new administrator, as well as a refresher or upgrade for the more seasoned school administrator.

THE PURPOSE OF THE BOOK

The purpose of this book is to provide school leaders with a concise, easy-to-understand synopsis of how three-, four-, and five-year-olds learn, as well as the tools to apply this understanding to early literacy. By providing sufficient background and insight into early literacy, it is hoped that principals, vice principals, and lead teachers will be able to support young children's literacy learning, assess the newest and latest trends and early literacy intervention strategies, and provide deeper and more meaningful programs so that children's literacy learning can be maximized during the early years. By providing the criteria for differentiating between practices that benefit young children and those that don't, it is hoped that principals will be able to promote practices that will make the most significant long-term differences.

Like the other books in this series, the focus of this book is on blending the theoretical with the practical in order to support school leaders in their instructional roles.

ORGANIZATION OF THE BOOK

This book has been divided into four sections for easy reference. Presented in a conversational format with real life examples, it offers school leaders both the background and tools that they need to implement sound early literacy programs. Chapter 1 and Chapter 2 outline, in easy-to-read terms, the information essential for understanding how young children learn, why particular programs are better suited for young children than others, and consequently, what makes a good literacy program. Chapters 1 and 2 provide the background information required to begin the conversation with staff about the nature of young children, their learning, and how school teams can best serve young children's preferred learning styles. Chapter 3 provides principals with the practical tools for working with teachers and school teams toward implementing and improving early literacy programs. Principals can use many of these tools for professional development, taking examples provided as models of good practice and working through the process of planning together. Chapter 4 reviews the essential keys to build a school team and school culture that will support and sustain good programs and ensure continuous improvement in early literacy.

SPECIAL FEATURES OF THIS BOOK

Each chapter starts out by asking one or two big questions and in response includes vignettes and examples taken directly from schools and classrooms. Checklists and templates—tools to assist school leaders as they work with staff—are provided in each chapter. At the end of each chapter is a summary and a few guiding questions that leaders can pose to staff as starting points for professional dialogue related to instructional practices in the early years. At the end of the book is a resource section titled "Tools for School Leaders," which contains many of the templates provided in reproducible form.

It is hoped that through this introduction to the world of three-, four-, and five-year-olds through the lens of literacy learning, you will discover the exciting potential of three-, four-, and five-year-old children's learning and the possibility of making a major difference in their literacy development. It is my hope that school leaders, having read this book, will be eager to get involved with our youngest learners, never hesitating outside the door of their classroom again.

CHAPTER 1

What Every School Leader Needs to Know About How Young Children Learn

The purpose of this chapter is to provide all school leaders—whether teachers, literacy coaches, or administrators—with the essential understanding required to develop effective literacy programs for three-, four-, and five-year-old children by addressing these two big questions: How do children learn? What are the essential qualities of a good literacy program?

The school leader will be introduced to the young child as a learner and the qualities to look for in literacy programs designed for young children. For if our goal is to positively affect the learning of young children, then the adults responsible for the education of young children have to understand the characteristics of learning in the early years—and that begins with the recognition that young children think, learn, and behave differently from older children and adults, and literacy programs that work for older children are not well suited to younger children.

YOUNG CHILDREN LEARN . . . DIFFERENTLY

Young children respond to open spaces by running to fill them up, to suggestions to pretend to be a snake by getting down on their bellies and making an "ssss" sound, and to building materials by attempting to pile and topple a tall structure.

Early educators and parents find out very quickly that they have to anticipate how young children are likely to respond to particular opportunities in order to effectively plan for eventualities. Educational theorist Kieran Egan (1997) describes three- and four-year-olds as prelinguistic (intuitive) and somatic (bodily-kinesthetic) beings. Children of ages three, four, and five years do not think in logical sequences; instead, they intuit meaning and respond with their bodies. Open space, such as a playground, a gymnasium, or a long open hallway, is interpreted as a place to be filled with big movements—such as running. A tower of blocks is ready to be knocked down with a kick or a hit. Active imaginations encourage young children to respond to almost any suggestion by playing the part.

Young children's evolving understanding of the world is also prelinguistic (intuitive) and somatic (bodily-kinesthetic). They learn through the somatic sensations of touch, gesture, building, manipulation, and movement that includes running, dancing, pretending, and role-playing. Their thinking occurs through their actions. Consequently these actions and experiences influence the development of more advanced neural pathways in their brain.

Many theorists have contributed to our current understanding of how young children learn and the characteristics of the stages of learning between ages three and six years (cognitive, social, moral, intelligence, language). In this first section, the reader will be introduced to some of the most significant theorists and their contributions to the field of early literacy.

Cognitive Learning

From theorist Jean Piaget (1896–1980) comes a foundational understanding of the cognitive capacities of children ages two through seven (what he called the preoperational stage). Young children are considered to be egocentric in their thinking, meaning they think others think like they do. Between the ages of four and seven years, they employ mental activities to solve problems, although their thinking is still largely intuitive: They are not conscious of their thinking or how they arrive at particular conclusions.

Piaget defined the concept of schema as an internal representation of the world based on external experience: This mental organizational or conceptual framework is the base from which new experiences are either assimilated or accommodated. The concept of schema has helped us understand the role that experience and background play in children's learning.

It is during the preoperational stage that children begin to represent their world using symbols that include words, pictures, and numbers. Young children develop the capability to pretend and assign living attributes to inanimate objects. Pretending is the necessary early stage of representation that later leads to using pictures, numbers, letters, and words to represent objects and ideas.

When developing programs for young children, it is important to design literacy experiences that create relevant literacy schema (e.g., through buddy reading), provide opportunities for representation of ideas through play and use of other symbols (e.g., through projects), and leave space in schedules for intuitive problem solving (e.g., through investigations). Examples of what this looks like are found in Chapter 2.

Social Learning

From theorist Erik Erikson (1902–1994) we are provided with insight into the stages of social learning: what he called "virtues" developed from social tensions. Depending on how responsive the early environment has been to a child's physical and emotional needs for food, comfort, and loving human contact, the child from birth to age two years will have navigated the trust-mistrust stage (the first stage of social learning) with either a sense of trust, security, and optimism or insecurity and mistrust. This is important to note because the outcome of this learning determines the approach children will take to the next phase of their learning.

Between the ages of two and four years, young children's social learning is focused on autonomy versus shame or doubt. During this stage, young children are motivated to try new things and to imitate adult behavior. Their desire to be autonomous means they will struggle at times against the rules set out by adults and are prone to tantrums and stubborn refusals when they do not get their way. This stage presents an ideal time for children to learn appropriate independence—to toilet and dress themselves and to learn small chores and basic routines.

From age three and a half years to formal school age, children are learning the social skills of initiative versus guilt. The healthy child learns to imagine, to cooperate with others, and to lead as well as follow. The challenged child is fearful, lacks social skills, depends on adults, and is limited in play skills and imagination.

A well-designed literacy program for young children acknowledges the need for children to be in a caring environment that supports their basic needs for warmth, nutrition, and comfort as well as appropriate autonomy and initiative. Young children need positive role models, choices, and opportunities, as well as time to try on new roles and behaviors without undue criticism. A literacy program that provides young children with rich experiences and gives them opportunities to represent their own evolving understanding of the world (e.g., through visual arts, drama, and music) allows young children to experience autonomy and satisfaction in themselves and in learning. Documentation and displays of children's thinking as outlined in Chapter 2 acknowledge this learning in visual and tangible forms.

Moral Learning

From theorist Lawrence Kohlberg (1927–1958) we discover stages of moral development based on his redefinition of Piaget's work. Kohlberg proposed that through their life experiences, children develop understandings of moral concepts such as justice, rights, equality, and human welfare. He determined that the development of moral judgment occurs over time and progresses through levels and stages. During the early years (the preconventional level) egocentrism limits the ability of the child to consider another's perspective. Actions are not so much determined by whether they are right or wrong as by the consequences. Children initially fear and avoid punishment, and this later translates into self-interest. Actions are morally relative, and children will interpret something for which they are punished as bad or wrong. Children follow the rules when it is in their best interests and negotiate deals in their favor.

According to Kohlberg, the way to teach morality is through moral dilemmas. Good literacy programs are those that are responsive to young children as developing moral beings and that provide opportunities for children to experience moral dilemmas and the tensions of good and evil, for example, through classic stories and mythic role plays as suggested by Egan (1997) and discussed in more detail later.

Learning to Be Intelligent

Theorist Howard Gardner's (1943–) study of children's styles of learning eventually led to the development of a theory of intelligence defined as a variety of styles used to solve genuine problems and make judgments that are valued in particular contexts or cultures (Gardner & Hatch, 1989).

Gardner's (1983, 1993) theory of multiple intelligences has transformed our thinking about intelligence; once limited in scope to language and mathematical proficiencies, we now understand intelligence to include multiple ways of knowing, which we all possess in various configurations. These ways of knowing include linguistic (words), logical-mathematical (reasoning), spatial (images, pictures, dimensions), bodily-kinesthetic (somatic sensations), musical (rhythms and melodies), interpersonal (bouncing ideas off others), intrapersonal (deeply internal), and naturalist (environmental orientation).

Young children need to have opportunities to re-present their growing knowledge of the world through multiple modalities. For each of the intelligences, there are particular ways of thinking and a particular approach to solving problems. Gardner (1993) calls these approaches "dispositions of learning." He recommends that children have opportunities to work with materials that evoke and provoke thinking along different lines. To be truly literate, young children need to apprentice in the literacies of all disciplines, including science, mathematics, art, technology, mechanics, music, history, social science, environment, and language and to learn from people who act as models or mentors and emulate these ways of thinking.

Having visitors perform tasks such as cooking, building, painting, or singing, while audibly describing what they are doing and thinking, using the rich language of their discipline, allows children to imitate these models as apprentices and build their intelligence as young children.

Language Learning

If we think of literacies as languages of different disciplines, we can apply our understanding of how children learn language to help us design literacy programs that encompass many different literacy forms. The environment plays a key role in determining the language or languages a child will learn. According to linguist Noam Chomsky, babies are hardwired to learn all languages; however, particular sounds, words, and phrases are reinforced by the world around them, determining which will eventually get used. Through exposure to a particular culture with particular languages, children's brains selectively delete some of this capacity, narrowing their imitation and learning to the language of the culture in which they are raised (Cogswell, 1996).

The period between eight months and six years of age marks a particularly rapid growth in language acquisition. It is estimated that by the time a child is three years of age, he or she understands 1,000 words or more and will acquire an average between 1,500 and 2,000 words before he or she is four years of age. With access to new words on a daily basis, the average child of three years has the capacity to learn four to six words a day. By the time a child is five years of age, the child's vocabulary has doubled, to between 4,000 and 5,000 words. This same child is likely to acquire another 3,000 to 4,000 words that year alone. Children's receptive vocabulary is much larger than their expressive language. By the time children enter formal school, they are using many different forms of communication to get their messages (thoughts and emotions) across. These messages can often be delivered without words. This example comes from a classroom of four- and five-year-olds.

Oliver skulks down the hall following his line of classmates, fist raised and finger pointed. Putting his hands together he takes aim. "Put that gun away!" I tell him, and he points his finger down, sticks it into his pocket and walks on.

Oliver, normally a timid child, does not always express himself well using words. It takes an astute observer to understand the ways he is communicating and to recognize the thinking that is going on without words. All too often, adults who do not recognize the capacity of the young mind assume that without words there is little thinking going on. Like their communication, young children's thinking is all action. We see this later when children begin to learn to read: They vocalize.

A well-designed literacy program recognizes that the building blocks for later literacy begin with rich literacy experiences that cross discipline, build vocabulary and background knowledge, and exemplify what it means to be able to effectively communicate in many modalities.

PLAY: A WINDOW INTO CHILDREN'S THINKING

Play is children's thinking made visible. For this reason, the observation of play is important to adults who want to understand what children are thinking, what they understand, and what they are in the process of learning.

> *Ben finds a stick on the ground and picks it up. He pokes it into a mud puddle and by dragging it creates a little river. Lunging forward, he stabs the stick into the air like a sword. Raising the stick above his head, he waves it like a flag. He drops the stick and jumps over it with both feet, leaving it behind him on the ground.*

Play usually begins with an object and an action. When Ben uses a stick to represent something other than a stick, he imagines. The ability to imagine changes Ben's relationship to reality. What starts as action on objects, ends in imagination, the development of a higher mental function. According to Vygotsky (1978), "The old adage that children's play is imagination in action can be reversed: we can say that imagination in adolescents and school-children is play without action" (p. 94). The latest research continues to link pretend play to the development of cognitive capacity. The value of play, besides the inherent value granted to it by young children, is that the complexity of play challenges the mind (young or old) to think and process in new and different ways, which leads to changes to the composition of the brain.

According to researchers Bergen and Coscia (2001), "Pretend play engages many areas of the brain because it involves emotion, cognition, language, and sensorimotor actions, and thus it may promote the development of dense synaptic connections" (quoted in Bergen, 2002). Pretend play requires the ability to transform objects and actions symbolically; it is furthered by interactive social dialogue and negotiation; and it involves role taking, script knowledge, and improvisation. Many cognitive strategies are exhibited during pretense, such as joint planning, negotiation, problem solving, and goal seeking.

Play takes many forms. Young children play with sounds, words, language, and music. Dress-up and pretend, drama, and movement are forms of play that draw children of three, four, and five years of age. Another form, typically found in early years classrooms, is play with different media. This form is particularly rich from an educational point of view because it makes children's thinking visible. Media that are easily manipulated, such as clay, paint, sand, and water, attract young children for this reason— they get to see their own actions on the world and thus their thinking becomes visible.

> *In the art area, Rachel is painting at the easel. She starts by painting a yellow sun, a red brick house, then people. She adds clouds and drops of rain, then more and rain until she has covered the entire page with blue paint. The sun, the house, and the people are no longer visible. When asked about her painting, she describes it as a rainstorm.*

In this example, Rachel's imagination leads and is led by the malleable paint medium that allows her to transform it and her thinking. Typically, children go through stages of manipulation with media based on their exposure and regardless of their age (adolescents must go through the same early stages with unfamiliar building materials as do four-year-olds). When children have opportunities to experience and play with a rich array of media over time, their expression of ideas and emotions develops both in complexity and sophistication. In early stages of painting, children will be able to represent only what their minds and their experiences allow; over time they will be able to control and determine end results.

For school leaders and classroom teachers, play is a tool we can use to assess what a child is thinking and a means for us to get the inside track on what the learner knows and is able to do.

When children are engaged in play with different media, we pay attention to their communication, including their acts of representation and their experiments with language. What are children representing through their play? Is there an attempt to do something new and inventive or to use more sophisticated vocabulary? When children play with mathematics materials, such as blocks, what words do they use to describe their actions or their construction (height, width, depth)? Through their actions, what do they show us about their understanding of the relationships between the various sizes and shapes?

If we think about language and literacy as developing along continuums from simple to complex, featureless to descriptive, basic to imaginative, indiscriminative to insightful, then how would you describe the child's use of language? Conceptually what does the child understand, what may be missing in his or her thinking, and how could his or her thinking be enriched or expanded?

Knowing what to do and how to support children's literacy development requires teachers who are astute observers interested in understanding and advancing children's learning about themselves and the world.

YOUNG CHILDREN LEARN LANGUAGE THROUGH SOCIAL INTERACTION AND INTELLECTUAL PLAY

According to Chomsky, learning the language of one's culture is a very complex process, requiring enormous creative and innovative potential, a genetic potential that is engaged with the right mix of social interaction and intellectual play (Cogswell, 1996).

It is only through active involvement with their environment (people, places, and things) that young children can construct meaning of the world in which they live.

Language is much more than sounds and words. Language is the tool of communication that we learn from the culture in which we live in order to engage others in social discourse (Vygotsky, 1978). Listen in as an infant "communicates" with her mother.

> *Three-month-old Mia responds to her mother Christina's smile and "hello baby" by moving her hands and producing an "ooo" sound, much to the delight of her mother, who smiles and repeats the sound "ooo."*

This interaction between Mia and her mom is a great example of social discourse. Young Mia wants to respond and has constructed a way of greeting her mother, one that goes beyond simply replication of sounds or a word, one that is filled with the animation and excitement at engaging with someone she knows and loves.

Young children learn to use different sounds and actions to elicit social interaction of different kinds; they cry to be picked up, smile to engage, and point to acquire.

In effective literacy programs, teachers engage in intellectual play with young children—extending their understanding—by providing the materials and means to explore their ideas, bringing new vocabulary into their play, and making authentic links to literacy.

LANGUAGE: THE EARLY FRAMEWORK FOR LATER THINKING

According to Vygotsky (1962), internal thought develops in a social context out of oral language. Vygotsky's book, *Thought and Language* (sometimes translated as *Thinking and Speaking*), establishes the explicit and profound connection between speech (both silent inner speech and oral language) and the development of mental concepts and cognitive awareness. According to Vygotsky, inner speech is qualitatively different from normal (external) speech. Language starts as a tool external to the child used for social interaction and as a kind of self-talk or thinking aloud. Gradually self-talk is used more as a tool for self-directed and self-regulating behavior.

> *Damia is traveling in the car with her grandmother, who points out the window at the scenery. Damia is interested in birds, so her grandmother points out different kinds. "Look at the birds, aren't they wonderful?"*
>
> *"Aren't they wonderful?" Damia repeats and then to herself, "One more time, aren't they wonderful?"*

In the end, "oral language and social speech becomes inner speech" (Vygotsky, 1987, p. 57).

The speech structures, mastered by the child, become the basic structures of his or her thinking. For instance, around the age of two years, the child learns that everything has a name, so each new object presents the child with a problem and that is to name it (Yardley, 1988). Early words and their meanings are the embryos for concept development.

How children think, and thus the language they use, is largely a function of the activities practiced within the social institutions of the culture in which they grow up—in other words, what they are exposed to. Those individuals who are significant to children, such as parents, teachers, and peers, have important roles to play in setting the stage for the development of young children's language and consequently the structure of their thoughts.

The structure of the language that a child habitually uses also influences the way the child perceives the environment. The structure of the language, the words the language has (or does not have), the importance placed on those words, and the meanings they convey provide a lens through which we view the world and can talk about it. Consequently, the more expansive the language base, the greater potential for more precise and more diverse thinking.

When children enter preschool or school, their world expands and so should the opportunities for them to discover, through language, more about their world and the people in it. The school leader has a key role to play to ensure that the language experience in schools is rich and complex, furthering children's understanding of the world and how it works. It starts with an understanding of the vast potential of the learner to learn. It happens by the selection of experiences, activities, and models that provide learning that is rich in nuance and meaning.

THE INTELLECTUAL BEHAVIOR OF YOUNG CHILDREN

The meaning that children attach to words changes over time with experience and reflection on experience. This is beautifully illustrated in the following example.

> *Victor, age 6, learning that it was his principal's birthday, asked, "How old are you?"*
>
> *"How old do you think I am?" the principal countered.*
>
> *"Seventy-two, like my mom," he responded.*
>
> *"Seventy-two?" the principal exclaimed in shocked tones.*
>
> *Victor paused and reconsidered, "I mean . . . twenty-seven."*

Children may attach the word *dog* to all four-legged animals, such as cows, and it is not until they have many experiences with four-legged creatures that they begin to refine their understanding of this word, by narrowing it to a specific species. As adults, we often assume that the meanings of the words we use are shared. We assume, incorrectly, that the child understands what we mean. And when children use a word, we assume that they have acquired the common cultural meaning of the word. However, children begin using words whether or not meaning is attached to them.

> *In a game of make-believe with Chris, I am sent away.*
>
> *"Banished," I tell her grandfather.*
>
> *Later he asks Chris, "Who was banished?"*
>
> *"Sharon was."*
>
> *"What does banished mean?"*
>
> *"I don't know," Chris says.*

For the most part, meaning starts with experience that becomes a memory or an image associated with a word. For example, the word *home* conjures up very different images for different people. Meaning also depends on the context in which the word is used. The word *blue* has many variations in tone and hue and is also used to describe a feeling, as in "feeling blue," or an event as "out of the blue."

So in school, if we teach *blue* simply as a word without its rich context, we simplify the word in ways that strip it of its possible meaning. We face the same dilemma when we teach the concept of shape and number. For example, if we use only one example when we teach the concept of three-sided shapes, the child's mental image of the concept of triangle is quite limited.

Literacy programs for young children must present the nuances of meaning in language, replicating the richness of conversation rather than lecture, allowing children the opportunity to try on new words and phrases to modify and revise word meaning over time while recognizing that these opportunities are the framework for children's later thinking about math, science, and more.

Opposites as a Way of Thinking

Young children first structure their physical world by opposites (hot/cold, big/little, soft/hard, crooked/straight, sweet/sour) as a way to orient otherwise bewildering, complex phenomena and bring order to their world (Egan, 1997). Egan cautions us to treat this categorization not as simple but as fundamental for understanding underlying issues and forces. He puts it this way: "Wisdom lies not in the knowledge of many things but the perception of the underlying unity of warring opposites" (Egan, 1997, p. 43).

Knowing that children think this way provides us with clues to effective classroom practices for educating young children. Providing experiences with a wide range of interesting and malleable media and exposure to stories that have universal opposites as central themes, such as male/female, brave/cowardly, good/bad, and permitted/forbidden, are perfect venues for children to explore opposites and opposing forces.

For only once children have categorized by opposites can they begin to understand degrees and variations. For example, a child may use the words *fast*, *slow*, and *speed*. However, to the child, speed means fast like a fast car. The child may not have a concept of velocity or variations in speed. In order to assess the child's understanding of the word, adults working with children have to pay close attention to both how words are used and what the child means by them.

Exposure to the experience and language of degrees and variations is important not only for expanding young children's understanding of the world but also for the language that describes it. For example, teachers of young children intentionally expose children to play with water that is hot, cold, tepid, warm, soapy, colored, and so forth. They provide opportunities for children to watch boiling water and learn about steam and evaporation, for if children don't experience these distinctions, they are not going to be able to talk, think, or write about them later.

Symbols Galore: More Than Print on a Page

Symbols are a form of shorthand that stands for the real thing.

Yardley (1988, p. 19)

In school, teachers typically think of symbols as pictures and print. However, to a young child, a symbol is anything that represents something else and is not the real thing. For example, in dramatic play, children use many symbols to represent other things: A block can be a phone, and beads can be food. When encouraged to play with symbols such as words, numbers, signs, diagrams, maps, songs, patterns, photos, miniatures, replicas, and other objects as intellectual toys, children develop deeper conceptual understandings.

If we want the child to know about something, for example Africa, then a picture, a book, or words won't do; the child must experience the real skins, fabrics, songs, and dances to understand something of the place. Trivializing or oversimplifying with the intent to teach limits comprehension (Yardley, 1988). The consensus in the research is that forcing the memorization of symbols before understanding risks conceptual understanding.

Words, by their nature, are limited. We know that words play only a small role in our communication—tone, facial expression, and body posture communicate much of what cannot be said. Through creative work and movement, children are more readily able to communicate their ideas. Children must be allowed to develop all means of expression, including music, movement, and art.

The Big Questions

> *In a kindergarten class, as the children are gathering on the carpet for a circle time, a young boy looks up at his teacher and asks, "You are not the boss of everything, right? There is still God and Jesus?"*

Young children ask the most difficult questions. At the age of three years, they ask questions such as "Why is the sky blue?" and "What happens when you die?" and "Where do I come from?" Contrary to the jokes made about adults responding to children's questions about where they came from by explaining about procreation (providing much more information than children really want to know), young children are sincerely interested in exploring the big questions. Children themselves bring many experiences to such discussions and much of these can be shared in a very matter-of-fact way. For example, a discussion of the death of a goldfish leads to conversations about the death of dogs and grandparents and the rituals of death and burial—things that children themselves have experienced. Young children's explanations, however, have elements of fantasy mixed in. For example, they may endow the dead with magical and supernatural powers. Their questions are the beginning stage of explicit inquiry. In her books, *Wally's Stories: Conversations in the Kindergarten, You Can't Say You Can't Play,* and *Kwanzaa and Me,* Paley (1981, 1992, 1995) discusses young children's growing understanding of concepts such as fairness, magic, and race and presents them in the context of a literacy-rich environment of inquiry.

The Role of Imagination and Magical Thinking

Between the ages of two and seven years, children think mythically. Their natural draw to fantasy, talking animals, and animals dressed in human clothing engaging in human activities is a further differentiation from opposites (Egan, 1997). Their apparent magical thinking is a way of making meaning and developing rules about how the world works.

Listen to young children's stories and self-generated narratives and you will recognize the story structure as having been built around the universal opposites of brave/cowardly, security/fear, love/hate, happy/sad, dominate/subordinate, rational/emotional, aggressive/passive, public/private, health/sickness, and poor/rich. We can use these opposites as vehicles to provide much richer curriculum than our current "intellectually impoverished set of topics focusing on local trivia and 'hands-on' activities" (Egan, 1997, p. 44). For we see binary opposites expressed beautifully and dramatically in the stories (folk tales and myths) of traditional oral cultures, which make these the perfect vehicle for capturing children's attention and imagination in the exploration of language. Young children understand concepts such as freedom and oppression because they experience these in the worlds of their family, classroom, and playground.

In the early years, story can be used to approach concepts and ideas typically reserved for later grades, such as history, science, and math, providing a rich foundation at a time when children clearly relate to and understand the underlying dichotomies provided through opposing forces. By using story as a teaching strategy, teachers can move beyond the simple traditional lessons on local community helpers to historical understandings of conflicts between races and nations (Egan, 1997).

We have the opportunity to provide children with a rich array of means to communicate ideas, including drama, dance, art, and music, as well as traditional modes of math, science, reading, and writing. Providing opportunities for children to express themselves through each of these means engages many intelligences and learning styles and allows children to exhibit their strengths as well as providing them with alternative languages to communicate their thinking and their feelings. The following is an example of how the elements of opposites, story, symbol, and expression might be used to create a meaningful literacy experience for young children.

When reading familiar tales such as "Three Little Pigs," the children create dramatic renditions of the anger of the wolf at being tricked, the fright of the pigs at losing their homes, as well as the expression of aggression and fear through movement. When the children reenact the story, words are held up as signs, ONCE UPON A TIME and THE END, embedding the meaning for the child with this experience and providing them with a tool they can use in other contexts.

Mythic Thinking: Story and Metaphor

The ability of young children to use and understand metaphor furthers our understanding of how they use language to make sense of their world in ways that take them beyond what is apparent to new levels of understandings. Gardner and Winner (1979) found that children aged three and four years fashion more significantly appropriate metaphors than children aged seven through eleven years. Preschool children's ability to use metaphor even exceeded college students' ability. Young children use metaphor effectively to help them understand something new or relatively unknown. Although their ability in this area surprises us and exceeds our expectations for young children, it explains why young children love stories so much.

It is the oral structure of stories, including rhythm, myth and metaphor, and the underlying conflicts, that captures the imagination of the child. We can safely conclude that to reach the young child, using these forms is the best approach. Educators must ensure that language opportunities enable young children to express their unique perceptions and consciousness. Language can also be a tool to enrich and enlarge their understanding and their aesthetic experience. The discipline to learn the conventions of language must be weighed against the freedom to play with and explore the limits of these conventions. The sensitive teacher recognizes that it is through play with the language and language structures of story that young children learn best.

EARLY LITERACY: IT'S MORE THAN SOUNDS AND LETTERS

By the time a child enters school he may already have a vocabulary of 10,000 words, a figure which doubles before he leaves primary school.

Yardley (1988, p. 11)

The rate of learning that occurs as children enter school is rapid. Yet the magical and fantastical thinking of young children tricks many adults into thinking that their thinking is simplistic and therefore instruction should be delivered in simple terms. Many literacy programs for young children focus on letters and letter sounds as the beginning step, and simple repetitive words such as color words and high-frequency words (*the, I, he, she, at*).

The difficulty with the simplistic approach is that it strips language and literacy of its rich meaning. Listen to a four-year-old's command of the language for a topic that he or she is fascinated with. Many a four-year-old boy can pronounce dinosaur names that adults struggle to pronounce. Not only is he likely to name the dinosaur correctly, he is likely to be able to provide you with details about its lifestyle, its unique characteristics, and its eating habits!

In order to develop rich programs and enriched literacy environments in school, school leaders need to be open to the potential of the young mind and think more along the lines of programs for the gifted and for enrichment, programs that include open-ended problems, and projects that engage higher level thinking.

Although the research related to play and cognitive development has been around for some time, it has had little impact on school practices. Time that may exist for play in schools is being eroded under the pressure for readiness for Grade 1. Complex social skills have given way to the teaching of isolated skills such as the alphabet, sounds, numbers, and colors. Principals need to be able to advocate for play as thinking and learning and to be able to differentiate meaningful play from time fillers.

Studies of the effect of play on literacy development indicated that embedding literacy materials within play settings shows increases in children's use of literacy materials and engagement of literacy acts (Christie & Enz, 1992; Einarsdottir, 2000; Neuman & Roskos, 1992; Stone & Christie, 1996). For example, Vukelich (1994) found that kindergarten children's ability to read print embedded in the environment was increased, and Bergen and Mauer (2000, cited in Bergen, 2002) found that children who had high levels of play with literacy materials in preschool were likely to be spontaneous readers of place signs and have greater pretend verbalizations in a "town-building" activity at age five.

Leaders in early literacy should resist policies that reduce time for social pretend play experiences in preschool and primary grades and work to increase funding for research on play/cognition relationships in early childhood.

CHAPTER SUMMARY

In this first chapter, the salient characteristics of the young child (age three to six years) as a learner have been captured, and the features of a responsive early literacy program have been elucidated.

Literacy learning at this stage is often misinterpreted as learning about sounds and letters and high frequency words. It is so much more! Characterized by opposites, metaphor, story, and the big questions in life, the thinking and the rapid language learning that occur between the ages of three and six years is the framework for thinking and literacy learning in later years. Young children develop the dispositions that lead to proficiency in various literacy forms through play in a rich array of linguistic, logical-mathematical, spatial, bodily-kinesthetic, musical, interpersonal, intrapersonal, and naturalistic experiences.

In this first chapter, the foundation has also been laid for identifying the qualities of a responsive literacy program, one that intentionally provides rich language experiences including modeling and engaging in literacy activities; building rich vocabulary from multiple disciplines; communicating through multiple modalities; using fantasy, story, and role play as the means to engage the young in moral dilemmas, binary opposites, and the big questions of life; and educating in the various dispositions required to readily engage in different disciplines, which include science, mathematics, arts, and languages.

QUESTIONS FOR DISCUSSION

- According to the text, what are the characteristics of the young child as a learner? What are the qualities of a responsive literacy environment?
- Identify some element in this chapter that you would like to learn more about.
- Compare and contrast what you have read in Chapter 1 to what we currently do or offer in our early years programs.
- Identify something that we could do in order to make our programs more responsive to the young learner.

C H A P T E R   2

What We Know Makes the Difference

In this chapter, elements of effective literacy programs are shared. Based on this information, it is hoped that school leaders will be able to distinguish between mediocrity and excellence when providing young learners with literacy rich environments. The focus of school leadership is assessing the school culture: identifying what it is and what it can become and working with staff to create the vision and move the school forward toward its goals.

This chapter addresses the following big questions: What are the elements of effective early literacy programs? And how do I as a school leader distinguish between those practices that make a difference and those that don't? At the end of the chapter, questions are provided for school leaders and school learning teams to use to assist them in developing an action plan for moving their school culture along the continuum of improvement toward excellence.

TRANSFORMING THE CULTURE: THE ROLE OF THE SCHOOL LEADER

Most significant in school leadership is the opportunity to shape the values and beliefs of teachers, in other words, transforming the culture of the organization (Fullan, 2005). Traditionally, programs for young children have been under tremendous pressure to become like the dominant school culture with its belief in and value for control, conformity, and a work ethic that translates into same age groups, whole group instruction, paper-pencil tasks, and quiet work.

Early years teachers are typically trained as generalist teachers with very little background in child development. Most of the professional development designed for teachers is subject specific and focused on the primary grades (Grades 1, 2, and 3). Without sufficient training in the pedagogy of the early years, teachers are tempted to look to publishers and published programs for answers as to what are the most efficient teaching strategies.

The principal, as instructional leader, has the opportunity to transform the school culture by asking pertinent and relevant questions and expecting something different. Some examples of questions include the following:

- What is our image of the young child as a learner?
- How will we determine the essential learning at this level?
- How can we build on the children's interest and engage young minds?
- What expertise do you bring to this problem?
- What are our greatest challenges at this level?
- What teaching strategies suit this developmental level?
- How will we assess learning through multiple means?
- How will we measure and monitor progress and communicate our success?
- How do we develop high hopes and expectations for all young children?
- How do we raise capacity and lay the foundation for later success?
- What sacrifices can we make to put children first?

ASSESSING THE PROGRAM: ONE SIZE DOES NOT FIT ALL

In elementary school, we act on the assumption that when children enter school, they come with similar language experiences, think in similar ways, and thus have the same readiness for the similar literacy experiences that we will provide for them at school. When we stop and think about it, it is not very likely that all children will have the same experience or be at the same stage of development at the same time. Yet educators act surprised when, for example, some children do not take to print as readily as others. In school, decisions about what to do when children experience difficulty in learning are for the most part determined by age and grade expectations. The design and structure of the school environment communicates a limited response, not because this is the way young children learn, but because the structures such as grouping by age and grade shapes educators' thinking.

Schools have traditionally been inflexible in response to perceived differences in children's learning, most often delivering more of the same rather than varying strategies to accommodate differences. Yet this "one-size-fits-all" approach contradicts virtually everything we have learned about effective teaching. When teaching is personalized and customized for the learner, all students benefit. According to Richard Allington (2001), in *What Really Matters for Struggling Readers: Designing Research-Based Programs*, students of all achievement levels benefit from exemplary teaching, but it is the lowest achievers who benefit the most (Allington, 2002).

The school environment has tremendous power to shape children's thinking about themselves as learners early in their school career, especially for those children who come from environments that are limited in the literacy experiences and opportunities. The design of the school teaches students what is important through what is placed on walls, what behaviors are modeled, what gets talked about, and what opportunities and resources are offered and provided. For example, a school that acknowledges only the work of the top students, who provides to struggling students outdated texts and worksheets while the upper groups get the new and most recent publications, sends clear messages about who and what is important.

To explain differences in children's learning or what we have come to call readiness to learn, home environments and general intelligence are often blamed. When young children come to school largely unprepared for the experiences they encounter there, educators tend to be sympathetic. Rather than acknowledging the learning children have acquired from their environment, learning that is different from the learning in school, their learning capacity is rated as limited or reduced simply because the learning does not come packaged in the school readiness form. As a result, we expect less rather than demand more when it comes to literacy learning. Children learn early on in their school career that they may not be very capable when it comes to school learning, and that message shapes their confidence and their willingness to take the risks required. Over time, these messages have a huge impact on their potential for later school learning.

High-quality programs for young children, such as Head Start, set goals of providing disadvantaged children with advantages rather than laying blame. These goals focus on enhancing children's development and school readiness; strengthening the family as primary nurturer; providing high-quality educational, health, and nutritional services; linking children and families to needed community services; and ensuring well-managed programs that involve parents in the decision making. Communication and agreement between preschool and school providers about the nature of early literacy and the expectations we have for early literacy learners are keys to success.

The guiding question for school leaders as they talk with teachers should be, "How are we meeting the diverse learning levels of the students in your classroom and in our school?"

RECOGNIZING THE EFFECT OF TEACHER PERCEPTION: THINK THEY WILL OR THINK THEY WON'T, YOU'RE RIGHT!

Results from numerous studies show that teacher perception has more to do with school success and school learning than socioeconomic and health factors (McCain & Mustard, 1999). Early studies on the effect of teachers' perceptions on student achievement support this idea of self-fulfilling prophecies: What teachers expect of students is often what they get!

When researchers led teachers to believe a subgroup of lower class students would achieve more rapidly than their peers, they did (as shown by increases in IQ scores) regardless of the fact that the selection of these students was random. The difference between these children and the rest of the class existed only in the minds of their teachers.

The High/Scope and Head Start programs in the United States have had tremendous success at giving disadvantaged three- and four-year-olds a step up. A year of intervention at home and school has paid off huge dividends in the long run with decreases in teen pregnancies and juvenile behavior and increases in completion of high school and further education. Besides building foundational skills, these programs influence how teachers in Grade 1 perceive how bright these children are, an effect that is long lasting.

From studies such as these, we can conclude that what teachers believe about the learning potential of the children they teach is paramount for what children will learn. Principals can learn a lot about how teachers think by the way they outline plans, construct lessons, communicate with parents, and assess learning.

- What terms do teachers use to describe children?
- Do teachers speak in terms of young children's assets or deficits?
- Who are the dominant players in the classroom? What is the balance between teacher talk and student talk? How is time divided between teacher-directed and student-directed activity?
- How is learning assessed—through checklists, anecdotal records, and portfolios?

Teachers who think in terms of deficits tend to be focused on what is missing. They view their teaching role as providing the information that is lacking. In their classrooms, time is dominated by teacher talk and teacher instruction. These teachers demonstrate wariness toward children's thinking. They expect children to replicate what the teachers do rather than come up with inventive or creative solutions. Assessment of student learning is often by checklists based on teacher-created criteria.

Teachers who are interested and awed by the learning that young children are occupied with, the background knowledge and experience they have acquired, and the connections they are making as they encounter new experiences demonstrate their interest in engaging children and advancing their learning by starting with student interest and providing children with experiences that extend their learning. They demonstrate a faith in the capacity of young children to advance in their learning. These classrooms are filled with student talk, student interests, and students engaged in their own learning. Assessments of student learning occur through a variety of means that include conversations, stories, models, photographs, and designs.

Identifying the model that teachers employ when planning for learning, whether one of deficit or asset, is an important first step for school leaders toward understanding the literacy program teachers are likely to design for young children. If teachers perceive the child through a deficit model, they are likely to expect and get less from children in terms of thinking and learning.

DEVELOPING THE EARLY DISPOSITIONS TO BE READERS AND WRITERS AND CRITICAL THINKERS

The effortless way young children learn to speak their native tongue surprises us, leading many to conclude that it must be a relatively simple task. However, when children fail to learn to read and write with the same effortlessness, we look for something or someone to blame. From a developmental perspective, by the time children enter school and are faced with the task of reading and writing, their rate of learning has slowed down. Reading and writing take more effort on the part of the child and a more deliberate involvement on the part of the adult.

The suggestion has been made that we should start earlier, at age four or before, to teach these fundamental skills, when children appear to learn more rapidly. However, a quick fix has the potential to do more harm than good. Since young children are so open and learning at a more accelerated rate, they benefit from rich rather than limited experiences in literacy, experiences that they can build on over time.

What we want to develop in children is the disposition to be readers, writers, and critical thinkers, which comes from a curiosity about and interest in the sound, rhythm, and music of language and text and the desire to communicate and converse, along with the propensity to do so. In the early years, the disposition to be literate first develops through sharing many rich social experiences with language and texts with parents and other significant people in their world. There still remains nothing more powerful for raising a reader than the interaction between a parent and young child with the child sitting on the parent's lap, turning the pages and pointing to the pictures as the parent reads the story aloud. A book in and of itself has little to no appeal to young learners. What has appeal is the shared experience and the interaction that, prompted by the text, happens before, during, and after the reading with a significant person.

CREATING THE CONDITIONS FOR LITERACY: SIX Ts FOR EXEMPLARY TEACHING

In schools, the challenge inherent in literacy instruction is to create conditions that motivate and support children to become literate. School leaders work at producing a school climate that supports teachers to continually improve on practices. Instruction is the key, and the principal's role is to develop policies that ensure that each year teachers become more helpful with learners. Based on observation of exemplary elementary classrooms in first and fourth grade, Allington (2002) developed the six Ts as criteria for effective elementary literacy instruction: time, texts, teaching, talk, tasks, and testing. In this section, each of these criteria is developed with examples for the early years classroom.

1. Time

In effective classrooms, time is devoted to children reading and writing about topics that matter to them. In less effective classrooms, more time is devoted to teacher's talk about books, to asking questions, and to prescribed assignments. In the early years classroom, large blocks of time (sixty minutes or more) are devoted to meaningful project work. At each station, students have access to good quality books and materials for representing and communicating their thinking. Children are actively encouraged to read and research information from books and assisted in recording their own ideas. They are provided time to represent their ideas through a variety of forms that include dramatic role playing, building, painting, creating, and experimenting with various media and materials.

2. Texts

Young children need books that appeal to them and pictures and symbols they can read accurately, fluently, and with good comprehension. In the early years classroom, these are good quality picture books that include fiction (fairy tales and myths), nonfiction (science and math), poetry and rhyme, familiar songs, wordless books, concept books, pattern books, big books, and recordings such as CDs and DVDs/DVRs. As well, they need books that address sexual, ethnic, and family differences and special needs. Environmental print and nonprint symbols are also provided as alternate forms of communication—these can include sounds, color, and light.

3. Teaching

In early years classrooms, teachers recognize that literacy learning does not occur in circle time when teachers are talking or at activities such as coloring. Learning occurs in small groups and in one-on-one sessions and side-by-side instruction when children are working with concepts and materials that make their thinking visible. This includes work with fluid media such as paint, clay, and sand where children can experience their thinking as an action. The teacher targets instruction for particular purposes by letting children in on the thinking that good readers and good writers engage in, and by providing direct, explicit demonstrations of the cognitive strategies that readers use when they read and write. Teachers model their thinking as they talk aloud and attempt to decode a word, self-monitor for understanding, summarize while reading, or edit when composing. For example, when a small group of children building a tower out of blocks are trying different strategies to make it taller, the teacher might reach for a resource book located in a building center and ask aloud, "I wonder how architects have designed tall towers?" Looking at some of the pictures, she might point examples out: "Oh, here is the Tower of Pisa, and it is tilting. That plan sure didn't work!" From there she might look for examples that demonstrate stability.

4. Talk

In the early years, teachers foster student talk. They encourage, model, and support purposeful talk that includes problem posing and problem solving. Teachers engage in higher level thinking with their students and extend their critical thinking by discussing ideas, concepts, hypotheses, strategies, and responses with one another. In the early years, teachers use question asking, not to get the right answer, but to make children's thinking visible. After story reading, teachers pose more open questions, to which multiple responses would be appropriate.

Question 1: What might happen if—?

Question 2: What other story have we read that had an ending like this one?

Question 3: Has anyone had a problem like the character in the story?

Teachers engage with children in their play, introducing rich and novel vocabulary to describe actions and to link play with literate activities through modeling.

5. Tasks

In the early years, classroom tasks are authentic and of longer duration. Authentic tasks are those that connect children to the natural world and the world around them. Children work with the same open-ended media, such as clay, blocks, water, and sand, over the course of the year in order to be able to explore and then manipulate them. Conditions of the materials such as sand are altered to further the children's thinking (wet, dry, coarse, smooth, etc.), enrich their vocabulary, and support their understanding of the natural world. Children may work on a writing task for days, and the writing gets revised over time; whole books are read and reread; individual and small-group research projects and inquiries are completed; and tasks integrate several content areas and year-long projects, such as caring for a garden or studying changes in water through different seasons.

6. Testing (Assessing)

In the early years, teachers assess student thinking along continuums of development rather than by simplistic outcomes such as the number of letters and sounds identified or how high the child can count. Portfolios of student thinking include visual representations (drawings, photos, narratives), videos of storytelling and drama, and audio recordings of talk and readings of written text both student and teacher scribed that represent student thinking over the course of one or two years. Elan LaMontagne (n.d.) displays the work of students in her class through a project titled "Building Things." For examples of her documentation go to www.youngchildrenslearning.ecsd.net/em%20changes.htm. This anecdotal qualitative evidence is fundamental to understanding the quality of the child's thinking, for developing purposeful lessons as well as recognizing growth over time and determining next steps in teaching. In *Observations and Reflections in Childhood,* Szarkowicz (2006) outlines how goals and next steps can be planned based on the observations of student work.

DEVELOPING AN INCLUSIVE LITERATE COMMUNITY: PROVIDING ONE-ON-ONE SUPPORT THROUGH MULTIAGE BUDDIES

The greatest challenge for principals and teachers today is the students whose skills do not meet the literacy norms or standards for their age or grade. With the compression of curriculum and the downloading of expectations, kindergarten and first-grade literacy expectations have become so finite that the pressure is on for children to be readers in kindergarten and first grade. When young children's reading skills don't match the requirements for the grade, failure and repetition is considered an option, despite the lack of research support for this strategy (Allington, 2001).

Notwithstanding the extensive research on peer tutoring and its well-documented benefits, whole group learning and graded groups continue to be the instructional norm in elementary schools. What may in fact be missing for readers at risk, many with limited home literacy experiences, are models of competency, intimate encounters with texts, and real contexts for developing skills to be nurtured, manifested, and strengthened. Katz (1995) suggests that what all children need are opportunities to observe and imitate a wide range of competencies with companions who match, complement, or supplement their interests in different ways. These are compelling reasons for principals to further their understanding of the role of peer tutoring and buddy reading with different-aged peers in elementary schools and scaffolding as an instructional strategy to promote literacy.

Developing Literacy Partnerships: Providing One-on-One Support

According to theorists such as Vygotsky (1978, 1985), the cognitive conflict that results during the interaction of different levels of understanding reaps intellectual benefit. However, instruction has to be designed above the student's current developmental level. Not only should the partners be on different developmental levels, the higher-level partner must be aware of the lower one's level (Driscoll, 1994; Hausfather, 1996, as cited in Riddle & Dabbagh, 1999).

The range of ages and academic levels found in public education provides a suitable setting for varied student grouping. Although the matching of older with younger students for the purpose of reading is a common occurrence in elementary schools, the practice has developed more out of the practical need for individual attention and reading support than any concerted attempt at theoretical understanding.

In theoretical terms, learning occurs in the zone of proximal development: the distance between the actual development (or what can be independently achieved through problem solving) and potential development (what can be achieved with guidance or collaboration; Vygotsky, 1978). This means that children can achieve much more with assistance from a peer or a teacher who can coach and provide strategies just slightly above the level they are currently working at. The guidance of adults or collaboration with more capable peers about the problem of reading bridges that gap for younger learners between what is known and what can be known (Riddle & Dabbagh, 1999).

For some, the idea of less- and more-skilled peers grouped together appears to be a watered-down approach in contrast to single-age groupings with the teacher as the expert. The chart that follows outlines the benefits for school leaders so they can present and support this as a preferred teaching strategy.

Multiage Groupings: Some of the Benefits for Learners

- Curriculum is multidimensional rather than unidimensional.
- Teaching strategies are diversified and new methods developed.
- Learning is continuous and children with a range of abilities have a place (gifted, disadvantaged, special need).
- Intellectual growth, understanding, thinking, and problem solving are augmented through cognitive dissonance (as children explain and argue points from different perspectives).
- Children have role models.
- Children are independent and interdependent.
- Children observe and imitate a range of competencies with companions who match, complement, or supplement them and their learning.
- Children learn by observing, exploring, imitating, experimenting, practicing, and applying.
- Children view themselves as proficient.
- Collaboratively, children achieve greater results than they would individually.
- Children typically achieve above their age/grade levels.
- Language use is generally more complex and versatile.
- Less proficient language learners develop sophistication in language use, complexity, and versatility.
- More proficient language users develop communication skills, adapting language to different audiences and different contexts.
- Children demonstrate patterns of leadership, group facilitation, and communication skills.
- Higher level thinkers learn to consider possibilities, explain what they think, and argue their position.
- Children learn skills of negotiation, argument, and cooperation.

Examples for School Implementation

The following segment provides examples of peer reading from an elementary school where peer tutoring and buddy reading is the norm (Speir, 2005). The examples include students in Grades 4, 5, and 6 paired with kindergarten-age students, kindergarten students with preschool children, and high school students with primary readers at risk. The examples are offered so that school leaders can develop a deeper understanding of what happens when different ages get together with reading as their purpose.

Example 1: Kindergarten With Grade 4 Reading Buddies

A quick walk through a reading buddy session taking place in the kindergarten room in an elementary school demonstrates many examples of kindergarten students working at different levels. Brooke is learning to attend to storybooks, Pieter is labeling pictures with words, and Raven is decoding text.

> *Samantha (Grade 4) sits beside Brooke (kindergarten) at a small table. Brooke is looking at the crowd of students reading together at tables and on the floor. She appears more interested in others than in the text. Samantha, normally shy and reserved, taps her on the arm to get her attention. When Brooke looks, Samantha continues reading from a book in front of them, following along with her finger under the text.*

During buddy reading, the older and younger students take on particular social behaviors, some of which are out of character. Samantha demonstrates redirection behavior in order to draw her buddy's attention away from the others and back to the book. She is letting Brooke know where her attention should be during reading, on the page and on the print. Samantha, normally hesitant, appears confident in this role.

Brooke, a student with special needs, has little regard for the activity of reading; yet while she is reading with Samantha, she experiences a strategy that she would not encounter on her own and is not likely to with an adult or much older peer. The sweeping of the finger under the text is a behavior that few older readers model once they have progressed to the more advanced visual sweep, yet Samantha, through her own reading behavior, models this intermediate step.

> *Ned, a Grade 4 student, sits beside Pieter, age 4, on the carpet. Ned points to the pictures at the bottom of the page and asks Pieter to find the objects in the picture of the park. "Can you find the slide?" Pieter has no problem.*
>
> *Looking at the picture of a fountain, Pieter asks, "Is that real water?"*
>
> *Ned says, "Yes."*
>
> *But Pieter doesn't think so. "The water in the fountain is real," he says, turning to face the water fountain in the room.*

The cognitive difference between two children's thinking is apparent when Pieter contrasts the picture of the water fountain to the real thing. Perhaps he is alerting Ned to the fact that he knows the difference. Perhaps he is continuing the activity of naming that Ned started.

> *Erin, a Grade 4 student, and her buddy, Raven, sit on their own at another small table. Raven holds the "A" book and Erin looks on. Raven is an advanced kindergarten reader. She is tracking the text with her finger, reading some of the small words and attempting to sound out the words she does not know. She gets stuck on the word* alligator.
>
> *"My mom says I am not supposed to look at the pictures," she tells Erin as she attempts to sound out the word letter by letter.*
>
> *"You can if it helps," Erin says matter-of-factly.*
>
> *Later when Raven stalls at the word* sleeping, *Erin asks, referring to the picture above the text of the alligator sleeping, "What is the alligator doing?"*
>
> *Erin gives her sounding clues, "The o makes an 'au' sound and those two letters [pointing to* ay] *make an 'a' sound."*
>
> *When they reach the words on the last page of the book ("an apple a day keeps the doctor away"), Erin asks, "Have you ever heard of 'an apple a day keeps the doctor away'?"*
>
> *Raven frowns and shakes her head, so Erin and the teacher attempt to help her understand how apples keep you healthy so you don't get sick and have to go to the doctor.*
>
> *When they finish their explanation, Raven smiles.*

Erin mediates the language gap between what Raven knows and doesn't know about the text in front of her. She alerts Raven to clues on the page that will help her understand the meaning and decode the text. Erin also teaches her about how the text works and how sounds go together in words.

As a consciously competent reader, Erin understands the complex task of reading and the need to employ multiple reading strategies. She herself uses many techniques and dismisses none when it comes to helping Raven learn to read, as shown when she suggests Raven can use the pictures if they help. She bridges the understanding gap for Raven when she explains the meaning of the colloquial phrase, "an apple a day," a saying Raven had not heard before.

Example 2: Preschool With Kindergarten Reading Buddies

Once a week, a small group of kindergarten children go across the street to the day care center for about 20 minutes to read to younger children. The kindergarten children, five- and six-year-olds, take three or four books that they select from the kindergarten class. These include books based on familiar songs, alphabet books, leveled reading books, and popular children's trade books. The interaction is less structured than the other programs. The children go with an adult from the school, sit on the carpet with their books, and wait for an opportunity to read with the day care children (ages three to six, some who attend kindergarten in other schools). This buddy program is a way for kindergarten children to become the experts and showcase their reading talents.

> *Victoria sits down beside her younger sister Amanda, age four, greets her with a hug, and opens the book she has chosen to read to her. "This is N," she says as she opens the book to the first page and begins to read the words on the page, from left to right.*

The visit to the day care center makes reading important for the kindergarten students. The reading starts with one book shared between two children and expands until reading fills the room. A young child from the day care sits down by the teacher, children go in search of books in the classroom, and another child snuggles up with a book and an adult.

> *Three boys, ages five and six, are hitting a balloon with plates. When the balloon drifts by where the girls are sitting, the teacher hits it. When it gets stuck on the ceiling, the buddies ask them if they want to read.*

Mark, the biggest boy, states, "I can't read." He notices the T book and grabs it. "I can read that," he says and opens the book. All three boys are now sitting facing the girls with books in between. Mark points to the word this *and says, "is."*

"This," Victoria prompts and Mark repeats her word, as he reads out, "This . . . is a train," word by word, finger pointing as he goes.

Soon Victoria is reading along with him, giving him enough time to read the word and filling in the words he does not know.

In only two visits' time, Victoria, age six, is demonstrating many of the behaviors of a buddy reader. Much as Sara, age 10, does, she tracks the text visually as the other child reads, allows wait time, gives clues, and supplies unknown words. She has likely learned some of these skills from the older and more competent readers that have coached her. Even though Mark and Victoria are the same age and attend kindergarten at different schools, in the context of the day care center, Mark is perceived as needing help, and Victoria is able to give it. For starters, she knows the books, and she demonstrates more proficiency in reading them. Both children accept these designations and take on the appropriate roles.

This is Haley's first day, and she is somewhat reluctant to read to the others. She has picked a simple pattern book titled Baby.

"Baby is drinking. Baby is eating. Baby is crawling. Baby is swinging. Baby is laughing. Baby is crying. Baby is sleeping."

She reads with little effort. She knows the pattern and is comfortable with the book.

These young kindergarten children have already learned many of the skills of reading, including book orientation (front and back, top and bottom, left to right) and some reading strategies (picture clues, first-letter sound, repeating text pattern, sight words, and contextual meaning), all meaningful and useful skills for reading. In the context of reading buddies, they integrate these skills seamlessly into their interaction. They rehearse in front of a receptive audience and take learning risks.

> *Haley takes the book* Wheels on the Bus *and sits beside Beth at the teachers' prompting. Beth is snuggled in beside a high school helper. Haley says she can't read it, so the teacher suggests they tell it instead, and she helps interpret the story by looking at the pictures. Haley sings the song when they get to the page with the musical notes.*
>
> *Victoria chimes in with phrases. When the teacher says, "The people on the bus . . ." she fills in, ". . . go up and down."*
>
> *"The babies on the bus cry . . ."*
>
> *". . . wa, wa, wa,"*
>
> *"The mommies on the bus say . . ."*
>
> *". . . sh! sh! sh!"*
>
> *As the final page is turned, Haley says, "The end," and there on the page are the words,* The End.

These young readers view their own reading behaviors as limited to particular texts. They express this perception freely, as Mark does, as he searches for a book he knows. When choosing books to take to the day care center, Victoria says that she can't read, until she finds ones that are familiar. She has picked books she knows and on the second visit, brings some of the same ones as she did in the first visit. Haley also comments that she cannot read *The Wheels on the Bus*. This perception of not being able to read or not being a good reader translates into reluctance with unfamiliar texts. Mark's perception of himself as a nonreader may come from the discrepancy between what others do when they read and what he cannot do. Is this not a prime example of Vygotsky's (1978) proximal zone and an opportunity ripe for scaffolding learning?

The comfort provided by having many opportunities to read familiar texts in different contexts and with different age peers (younger and older) is important for building students' confidence as readers, but more important, it allows students to match, complement, or supplement their learning (Katz, 1999). Each reading takes a different tact, as observed when Victoria reads the *Arthur* story, a story she rehearsed with her teacher and that she now reads confidently to the other children.

Last week, Victoria read Arthur's Reading Race *to the other children with help from her teacher. Today she reads it word by word to one of the boys. She points to the environmental signs in the illustrations (Zoo, Gas, Taxi, Milk, Don't Walk, Keep Off the Grass). On the second to last page, there is a sign on a park bench that reads "Wet Paint," and on the final page, the back of Arthur's blue jeans are white because he sat in the paint.*

Tony, who has not been following this story, listens to the children talking about what happened at the end of the book. He asks to see the sign, so Victoria turns back one page and shows him the sign, "Wet Paint," and then turns back to show him the illustration of Arthur's white pants.

The teacher asks the question, "Do you think that Arthur can't read, or does he just not follow rules?"

"Follow rules," Victoria says and she turns the pages of the book back to where Arthur is standing on the grass and the sign reads, "Keep Off the Grass."

When the children review and discuss the ending to the story *Arthur's Reading Race*, Victoria addresses Tony's comprehension question. She even provides evidence from the text, a skill promoted as a response strategy in later grades. Moving this distance from comprehension to discourse about the text is prompted by a question about whether Arthur had a problem reading or just following rules. Victoria's response raises the question: Now that she is a reader, can she imagine what it is like to not be able to read?

Example 3: Grade 1 and 2 Students at Risk With High School Reading Buddies

This peer-tutor program started several years ago as a partnership between the special education teacher at the elementary school who was looking for support for students in social, literacy, and numeracy skills and the teacher at the high school who was teaching a parenting course. Classroom teachers at the elementary level identify students, ages 6 to 10, who they think might benefit from having a peer tutor. Before the program begins, the teachers from both schools meet to match the tutors to peers, based on criteria that include gender, social skills, and academic abilities. With rare exception, the pairs continue to work together throughout the year. The elementary children identified by the teachers lack reading readiness. At the beginning of first grade, they often lack the fundamental knowledge of basic literacy skills (alphabet and letter sounds), rely on memorization of patterned text, and display a lack of interest in reading.

At the beginning of each semester, the elementary staff meets with the parenting class to provide training on strategies for how to support young children as readers: how to select books, how to read to younger children, how to plan reading strategies for learning to read, how to assess sight vocabulary, and how to devise word games.

Tutors and peers meet once a week, first thing in the morning or afternoon on different days of the week, according to the high school schedule. A typical session lasts about 40 minutes and is composed of four activities: reading familiar books at the child's independent reading level, word study including sight word review and playing word games, being read to from a book selected by the tutor, and shared journal writing.

> *High school students greet their peers outside their first- and second-grade classrooms. They tower over their tiny buddies. They walk in pairs, one big and one little, down the hall, and find an empty spot to sit together on the floor. The younger students hold their "Just-right" books contained in the bottom half of decorated cereal boxes. The tutors have books, too, ones they have chosen from the town library to read to their peers. The noise subsides as their focus shifts from each other to the books in their hands. A high school tutor, sitting close to his peer asks, "Do you want to read first, or will I?"*

Elementary teachers rate the program as successful because of the one-on-one attention and the academic support that their students receive when working with a peer-tutor.

> *Daniel, a Grade 1 student, turned away from his tutor at their first meeting in the library, uninterested in him and the questions he was attempting to ask him. Now he lies on the floor on his belly beside his tutor, working for him on a reading activity.*
>
> *A high school student, whose attendance is poor, comes on the days when we have peer tutors.*

Teachers consider the academic benefits of reading to be of primary importance. On their midterm assessments, teachers note gains in reading levels and sight word acquisition for the Grades 1 and 2 students. Almost all the Grade 1 children progress by one to three reading levels, with the greatest gain in reading occurring for two Grade 2 students who progress six to seven reading levels.

The intention of mixed age groups is to "increase the heterogeneity so as to capitalize on the differences in the experience, knowledge, and abilities of the children" (Katz, 1995, p. 2). Ideally, every elementary child would be involved in such groups and every child, through different matches, would have the opportunity to play the role of both expert and novice. Regardless of skill level, each child benefits from experiencing both roles, actions that, in and of themselves, require moving out of one's zone of comfort and into another's, whether on a social, academic, or intellectual level or any combination of these.

Socially, these buddy-reader programs provide a zone of safety where students can take on different social roles, regulate their behavior, and accommodate for differences. Opportunities are provided for students not only to understand their own learning but also to identify the stage of learning that others are at and learn to accept the differences.

Academically, it can be argued that taking on the role of the expert and the novice, in different contexts and with different people, by the very nature of the act, challenges students in the proximal zone. In their pairs, children progress in their reading and reading skills. They begin to recognize reading on a continuum, as a lifelong process with many points and supporters along the way. They can identify their progress and the progress of others more consciously and celebrate personal bests.

Intellectually, the context of elementary school offers an authentic setting for reading as a shared activity within a community of learners. School leaders can expand this opportunity by creating schoolwide and grade-specific projects that will engage learners in the pursuit of knowledge, provide them with a reason and a voice to share what they are learning, and help them develop a social conscience, thereby taking this pursuit to higher levels and into broader contexts.

For our youngest learners, the opportunities to have models of competency, to have intimate encounters with texts, and to experience real contexts in which their individual developing skills can be nurtured, manifested, and strengthened through buddy reading appear ideal.

The myth that the classroom teacher is the only reading authority must be dispelled and replaced with wider images of the teacher as coreader and facilitator and including students as co-collaborators and reading experts. Providing time and permission for students to sort through the differences in their thinking, to explain, and to argue is also a necessary component of a thinking curriculum.

According to Vygotsky (1978), an essential feature of learning is that it awakens a variety of internal developmental processes that are able to operate only when the child is in the action of interacting with people in his or her environment and in cooperation with peers (Schütz, 2004).

The review of such strategies contributes to our understanding of social learning theory as it is applied in the context of buddy reading and peer tutoring in an elementary school. It underscores the importance of a balance among the social-emotional, academic, and intellectual goals recommended by Katz (1999) to ensure the benefit is for our youngest learners.

For principals, what is important is recognizing that single age groups rarely provide students with the support they require to learn new skills. Principals can support the mix of ages by actively seeking and encouraging learning partnerships between different age and skill levels in the school and within the school community to support literacy projects.

STRATEGIZING FOR A MORE FLEXIBLE CURRICULUM

Most teachers in elementary classrooms understand what is meant by the term "teachable moment." During lessons, teachers seize opportunities when a student presents an idea or asks a question that will further the thinking or explain a concept in another way. Teachers, in their planning, attempt to catch age-appropriate interests and bring something from the world of their students into the classroom as motivators for learning. The negotiated or flexible curriculum takes the idea of the teachable moment a step further by encouraging teachers to develop units of study that focus on the children, their interests, and their world. The idea of the negotiated curriculum comes out of the work with preschool children in Reggio Emilia, Italy, where early years teachers are documenting and studying children's work and developing plans based on the analysis of children's learning. The following quote explains their thinking.

> The curriculum is not child centered or teacher directed. The curriculum is child originated and teacher framed. We have given great care in selecting the term "negotiated curriculum" instead of emergent or child centered curriculum. We propose that "negotiated curriculum" better captures the constructive, continual and reciprocal relation among teachers, children and parents and better captures the negotiations among subject matter: representational media and the children's current knowledge. (Fyfe & Forman, 1996, p. 4)

The Negotiated Curriculum

The idea of the negotiated curriculum bridges the gap between the *taught* and the *learned* curriculum. School leaders have come to understand that the focus on teaching often fails to recognize what the child already knows, but more importantly ignores the child, who is in the process of making his or her own meaning from the learning environment. Recent books in curriculum reform highlight this recent shift in curriculum from a focus on what is being taught to a focus on what is being learned. The idea of a negotiated curriculum takes us to yet another place, the space between the teacher and the child that builds on the interests and propensities of the child and the goals of curriculum. Topics for study can come from many places, including but not limited to children's questions and talk, community or family events, as well as children's interests (puddles, shadows, dinosaurs, etc.).

Team planning is an essential component of the negotiated curriculum. Teachers work together to formulate hypotheses about the possible directions of a project, the materials needed, and possible parent and community support and involvement. School leaders facilitate and support team planning by coordinating and providing opportunities for teachers to meet.

The multiple forms through which concepts are presented and documented are also essential, including print, art, construction, drama, music, puppetry, and shadow play.

This means that school leaders have to help teachers redefine their roles as teachers from "sage on the stage" to "guide by the side" where skills of negotiation, collaboration, collection, and documentation and analysis become more important and relevant.

In Chapter 3, some examples of negotiated curriculum are developed as lessons and unit plans.

DEFINING THE TEACHER'S ROLE

Instruction Versus Construction of Knowledge

Principals need to be aware of the ongoing debate that plays itself out in programs for young children between instructivist and constructivist methods and the effect on literacy. The instructivist method typically occurs in schools, especially in later grades, where the focus is on the teaching. The constructivist approach typically occurs in preschool and the early years, where the focus has been on children learning. However, in recent years, as curriculum goals are compressed, kindergarten and Grade 1 are becoming more instructive in their orientation.

The instructivist approach focuses on instruction and the acquisition of useful and meaningful skills. Goals tend to be structured, sequenced, and decontextualized, requiring some group or individual instruction in order to achieve mastery. Tasks involve memorization of symbols, responding to questions with correct answers, and practicing routine tasks. At the kindergarten level, reading and writing is interpreted as forming letters and learning sounds, so we see phonics and phonemic approaches being widely used. The teacher-instructor is of primary importance, playing the dominant role in the classroom. The strategy for children coming from less literate environments is to instruct them on the conventions of text (sounds, letters, and words) and low-level comprehension (retelling).

Contrast this to the constructivist approach, rooted in the early educational theorists, with a focus on learning and the child's construction of knowledge. Goals tend to be thinking-oriented, addressing dispositions or habits of mind, such as making sense of experience, theorizing about cause and effect, hypothesizing about observations, or analyzing and synthesizing information. These most often occur when children are involved in investigations. In these classrooms, ideas come from various sources, and sometimes the best teacher is not the adult. Peers learn from one another, and peers learn from students with different abilities. When children have the opportunity to practice with older and younger and differently abled peers, they accomplish things they would not be able to do on their own. Higher-level thinking prompted through challenges and projects move thinking up the ladder of Bloom's taxonomy, from knowledge (name), to understanding (explain), application (demonstrate), analysis (compare), synthesis (design), and evaluation (judge; Bloom, 1981).

Katz (1999) argues for intellectual goals in early childhood, citing studies that show that preschoolers, especially boys, who attended programs that were constructivist in nature fare better in school.

"Longitudinal studies comparing instructivist and constructivist approaches suggest that early gains of children in the instructivist preschool curricula do not last more than a year or two" (Katz, 1999). Further, Katz and others have concluded that the disposition to be a reader can be damaged by premature instruction.

For principals, this means we need to work with teachers to develop literacy programs for young children that utilize a constructivist approach, ones that recognize and encourage children to develop the dispositions of readers and writers and critical thinkers. Through purposeful investigations, we develop habits of mind that will have long-lasting effects. Early in Chapter 3, a strategy for selecting purposeful investigations is provided.

Teacher as Researcher, Co-investigator, and Partner in Learning

> The saying in educational circles goes, "in secondary school we teach subjects, in elementary school we teach children." Adding to this, "in the early years, we learn from children."

The early years teacher takes on a collaborative teacher-learner role as he or she researches, co-investigates, and partners with children in their learning. Simply put, the *teacher as researcher* means teachers learning to pay attention to children's learning in order to determine how and what to teach.

As partners in learning, teachers of our youngest learners learn from careful and attentive observation of children engaged in their learning. These educators carefully listen, observe, and document children's work and the growth of community in their classroom (Edwards, Gandini, & Forman, 1998). The early years teacher is a devoted and attentive student of children. This teacher dedicates a lot of energy to listening to the child, observing, taking notes, and recording conversations between children. While knowledgeable about subjects, he or she does not impose knowledge on children but rather contrives situations ripe with learning potential so that children will learn what can rarely be taught.

An example comes from a kindergarten classroom where a visit to the local art gallery serves as the starting point for a variety of follow-up learning activities in the classroom. Children are given opportunities to reconstruct their knowledge of the art space through their play.

After studying and analyzing the thinking of children, the teacher takes her cues from the actions of the child. She provokes ideas, stimulates thinking, and encourages collaboration with peers.

The teacher listens to the children's ideas and their questions and then provides the resources to allow the children to take their learning to new levels. She brings artists into the classroom to demonstrate their craft and to engage children as apprentices in artworks. The teacher provides access to examples of different types of art (including abstract, pointillism, surrealism, impressionism, and realistic art) and materials (brushes, rollers, printing blocks). Children name and display their work in art gallery style and invite parents, grandparents, and neighbors to view their work. They act as gallery guides, explaining the artworks, how they were made, what they are named, and how they have been interpreted.

The interaction between teacher and children and the development of ideas is ongoing. The teacher is continually committed to understanding young children's thinking and reflecting on his or her own teaching and learning.

From the Learning Center (http://www.tlcofdrphillips .com/curriculum.htm) Reggio Emilia approach, we glean this interpretation of the teacher's role based on the Reggio Emilia philosophy:

- Coexplore the learning experience with the children
- Provoke ideas, problem solving, and conflict
- Take ideas from the children and return them for further exploration
- Organize the classroom and materials for learning and to be aesthetically pleasing
- Organize materials to help children make thoughtful decisions about the media
- Document children's progress: visual, video and audio recordings, portfolios
- Help children see the connections in learning and experiences
- Help children express their knowledge through representational work
- Form a collaboration between other teachers and parents
- Have a dialogue about projects with parents and other teachers
- Foster the connection between home, school, and community

Studying Children's Thinking: The Inquiry Process

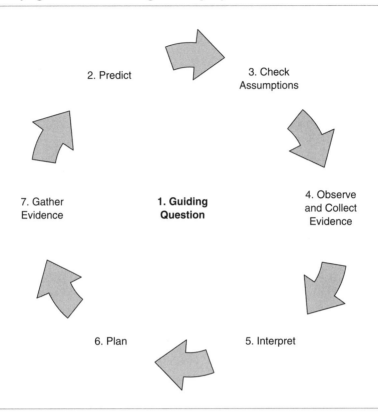

The chart above outlines the steps a teacher takes when developing and working through an inquiry into children's learning. Following the chart, an example is developed from a study of light and shadow.

1. The inquiry or classroom research begins with a guiding question (e.g., What do these children understand about light and shadow?).

2. The teacher makes predictions (forecasts) about what the children will know and want to investigate (e.g., I think they will know something about reflection, be interested in refraction, and love shadow play). These predictions help develop a focus on what to observe.

3. The teacher checks assumptions by providing materials so that children can explore their thinking (e.g., flashlights, water, mirrors, fabrics, puddles, light tables with ink).

4. The teacher observes the children play with these materials and records observations as evidence. This includes multiple representations using different media (e.g., photos, videos, scribed language, diagrams and pictures drawn by the children).

5. With a teaching partner, the teacher examines the collected evidence and interprets it (e.g., the children are getting the idea of light traveling through things and think that the water bends the light; are there other materials I could use to develop this thinking?). This collaboration reduces subjectivity and a single-perspective analysis.

6. The teacher makes plans to develop children's thinking by introducing different materials, challenges, and real life examples (e.g., puddles, aquariums, fountains, hoses, and sprinklers).

7. The teacher gathers additional evidence of children's work and displays it (e.g., a display in the hallway showcases photos of the children's experiments with light and their scribed conclusions).

Designing the Classroom Environment

The classroom environment can be considered to be a second teacher. The teacher carefully organizes space for small and large group projects and small intimate spaces for one, two, or three children. Documentation of children's work, plans, and collections are displayed both at the children's and adults' eye level. Common space is made available to children from different ages to come together. This might include the dramatic play areas and worktables for children. For some inspirational photos of classroom space design, go to the North American Reggio Emilia Alliance Web site (http://www.reggioalliance.org). Also explore the article and photos by Patricia Tarr (2001) at www.designshare.com/index.php/articles/aesthetic-codes-in-early-childhood-classrooms/ on the DesignShare: Designing for the Future of Learning Web site.

Designing Learning From Peers

Peers can be considered to be a third teacher. In any class, there will be a range of stages and levels of proficiency in various stages of literacy development. These stages tend to be quite uneven in the early years. Teachers capitalize on these differences by intentionally grouping children to maximize the use of experts and novices. Children learn from each other in ways they cannot learn from an adult. Vygotsky's (1978) theory of proximal development suggests that peers who are closer to the level of the child may be in a better position to teach something than an adult who is far removed from the learning. The buddy reading examples from an earlier section of this chapter are good examples of peer teaching and learning.

> *Samantha (Grade 4) sits beside Brooke (kindergarten) at a small table. Brooke is looking at the crowd of students reading together at tables and on the floor. She appears more interested in others than in the text. Samantha, normally shy and reserved, taps her on the arm to get her attention. When Brooke looks, Samantha continues reading from a book in front of them, following along with her finger under the text.*

Documenting Young Children's Thinking

Listening to children's talk and paying attention to their actions as they engage with different media provides many insights into what children already know and the knowledge they are in the process of constructing. Documentation of children's work-in-progress is an important tool in understanding and comprehending the learning process for the children themselves, their teachers, and their parents. When teachers record children's descriptions and their stories about their play over time and compare these, they begin to understand children's thinking as a work-in-progress. They then find the entry points for conversations, complementary materials, stretching experiences, and new vocabulary to describe their work. When these recordings of work are shared with the children and their parents, they become the starting point for dialogues about the work, the child's thinking, and how it is being expressed at home and at school. This naturally leads to consideration of next steps, for example, what other perspective or point of view might advance the child's understanding.

Photos of children engaged in experiences, alongside their words as they discuss what they are doing, feeling, and thinking, are displayed as graphic presentations of the dynamics of their learning (bulletin boards, portfolios, collections).

Collections of photographs, pictures, print, art, construction, drama, music, puppetry, and shadow play serve as wonderful examples of the types of visual representations of children's thinking that are possible. Displays, or exhibits such as *The Hundred Languages of Children,* visually present for visitors young children's powers of thinking. The drawings of these four-year-olds look more like what we would expect from the drawings of twelve-year-olds. The *ReChild* publication from Reggio Emilia provides some examples of the work these children are engaged in. This information can be found at http://zerosei.comune.re.it/pdfs/rechild08.pdf. The exhibit travels around the world, and the schedule can be found at http://zerosei.comune.re.it/inter/reggiochildren.htm.

Features of Effective Documentation

- Is focused on a specific question about learning
- Represents a continuum of learning: focusing on processes as well as outcomes
- Like a narrative, tells a story of what goes on in the classroom
- Takes multiple forms in order to capture different dimensions of learning (words and pictures capture understanding, photo and audio capture social and emotional dimension, reflections and analysis capture meaning)
- Is a public display, making group learning and group identity visible to parents, peers, and teachers
- Involves collaborative analysis and self-assessment; it helps children understand their own learning
- Shapes future learning
  (Project Zero, Harvard Graduate School of Education, 2006)

Principals ought to know that the progress of children's thinking is for the most part a function of the teacher's actions and design of the environment. The inquiry approach taken by teachers toward understanding, documenting, and responding to children's thinking furthers and advances childrens and teachers' thinking.

Planning Projects and Investigations

One way that teachers and principals can develop children's thinking over time is through ongoing projects and investigations. As previously mentioned in Chapter 1, young children are naturally curious about the big questions in life, such as, Why is the sky blue? What happens when you die? Who is the boss and why? They also notice and pay attention to small details such as a ladybug in the grass or the contours of a small stone. Projects and investigations of topics worthy of children's attention and effort have the potential for engaging and sustaining young children's interest over time. The benefit is that children then are given the time to construct and reconstruct their conceptualizations of particular phenomena and to develop shared meanings. As already cited, the study of puddles or shadows is rich with scientific potential. Out of the study of the puddle and shadows come diagrams, experiments, information, and procedural texts.

The provision of authentic social contexts for reading about authentic issues and related to authentic projects is key. Creating a broader definition of reading is important, one that includes not only a wider variety of reading materials, but also experiences with reading that provoke, by their nature, higher level thinking. Investigations and projects such as saving threatened species or supporting victims of floods and natural disasters are recent examples of concerns that elementary students relate to in authentic ways.

Building on the Oral Traditions

Prelinguistic cultures use rhythm and narrative as tools for remembering and meaning-making: learning things they will later understand. Children also start by learning the whole and then breaking learning down into parts. Stories and rhymes told to the beat of a drum are recalled before the sounds and words make sense.

The basis for any language starts in the oral traditions: the songs and the word plays between mother and child; the rhymes and rhythms of the playground; the traditional stories passed down from one generation to the next; the narratives that shape a culture and a society. Before children can understand print on a page, they must understand the words and their meanings within the context of the culture in which they live. Before children can think critically about what they are reading, they have to have discussed the meaning and the implications. Before teachers can know what meaning children attach to particular words or phrases, they have to engage children in dialogue and listen to their explanations as they engage with materials, ideas, and others.

The best literacy classrooms are filled with student talk, purposeful talk that relates to problem posing and problem solving, talk that makes the children's thinking visible. The best classrooms are filled with conversational talk and open-ended questions that allow for multiple responses rather than interrogational and confrontational talk that leads to narrow responses. Teacher expertise is key, for more thoughtful classroom talk leads to improved reading comprehension, especially in high poverty schools (Allington, 2002). In the most successful classrooms, talk is personalized, providing particular responses to students and the particular problems they pose.

Story and Storytelling

The talk of children often takes the form of stories. Good teachers capitalize on this talk as the foundation for classroom learning. Principals can support teachers' and children's storytelling as a legitimate means of meaning making, recognizing that we all tell stories as a way of participating in culture that is above all else social. Sometimes this requires courage and insight, since children's storytelling can at times walk at the edges of social acceptability.

Children naturally engage in storytelling about their lives and from their imaginations. Storytelling is the way that young children think and the way in which they enter into public dialogue and negotiate the socially established structures of meaning in their society, whether that be a group of peers, a classroom, a family, or the larger community. It is not uncommon for young children to present preposterous ideas (from an adult's point of view) to see how they will fly in the group. Will they be accepted? If so, the author is empowered to tell again. Through story and storytelling, young children invent and reinvent their lives.

Through storytelling, children learn the power of words as they capture the audience's attention and change predictable story outcomes. Through storytelling, children develop identities and make connections with other characters, sometimes as the hero, the helper, or the mom.

Using children's natural affinity for storytelling as classroom texts leads to discussions about the problems and issues the children are working through, such as fairness and magic, and the teacher as researcher gets an insight into how young children think about these topics. Paley (1981, 1992, 1995) embodies this role as she scribes individual stories in her classroom during group time; the author (the child whose story has been scribed) chooses a cast (children from the class) to act the story out. She also uses stories such as picture books and fairy tales to provoke children's thinking, and she creates her own stories for the same purpose. In her books, Paley explores issues and problems that are relevant to her as a teacher-researcher and to the children in her class; in *You Can't Say You Can't Play*, she explores social relations and exclusion, and in *Kwanzaa and Me*, she explores race. Through her own story of *Princess Annabella and the Black Girls*, she creates the space within her classroom for young black girls to develop representations of black princesses, replacing the dominant white images that pervade their drawings and dramatic play. In this way, Paley explores identity and challenges prejudice. In her classroom, story is a vehicle for children to experience culture, identify with characters that are like them, and to develop an understanding of those who appear different.

DEVELOPING LITERATE RICH ENVIRONMENTS AT SCHOOL

In order to develop literate rich environments, teachers need to be very conscious about what they choose to put into that environment. The following list provides some suggestions for basic ideas and materials. Principals will want to support the development of rich literacy-based materials as the foundation for later literacy learning. Note: The following list can also be found in the "Tools for School Leaders" at the back of the book as a reproducible checklist (Tool 1).

A literate rich environment

- emphasizes open-ended responses to a variety of experiences;
- includes environmental signs and labels displayed at the eye level of children for functional purposes (open, closed, children's names);
- includes sign-in and sign-up sheets;
- includes white boards with markers and magnetic letters and words;
- provides many good quality books, audiobooks, reference books, handmade books, children's scribed stories, and books in all areas of the room;
- provides books, stories, and songs that reflect children's experience and the experience of others (including culture and ethnicity);
- encourages daily stories, books as starting points, and books as references;
- includes chart stories;
- includes recorded questions;
- provides paper and pencils in all areas of the room; and
- provides aesthetic media (scarves, streamers, musical instruments, paint, clay, art materials, and dramatic play props).

BUILDING PARTNERSHIPS WITH PARENTS

We clearly know that it only takes one significant person in a child's life to guarantee success at school. This significant person communicates the value of learning and education and is often a parent or grandparent. For these reasons, it is important to involve parents in their child's education early and to sustain this relationship over the time they are in elementary school. Parents who may not have advanced literacy skills most often welcome support when the school coordinates it, while maintaining the belief that their child can achieve. Schools have to find ways to bridge communication gaps between languages and cultures by providing interpreters and hiring staff that reflect cultures and the community. Principals have a key role to play in valuing this relationship with parents and communicating its value to staff and to the community.

Inviting Parents Into the School

Parents are children's first teachers and yet are still often intimidated by the classroom structure and fear the comparison of their child and their parenting to others. Parents need to be invited into the classroom to share in the learning going on there. Open houses for events that showcase and celebrate children's work are great opportunities to have parents visit and participate in their children's learning at school. Art galleries, museums, portfolio nights, and video nights are some examples.

Parents Share Their Expertise and Their Culture

Parents can be welcomed into the classroom as experts or visitors, to show off their new baby or a talent, hobby, or job. Parents can read and be read to by children in the class. Parents also provide an extra pair of hands for activities that require more intensive help or supervision. In multiethnic neighborhoods, parents can bring their culture to school, sharing foods and cooking experiences, stories, art, and music.

Library and Reading Connections

Regularly scheduled visits to the school and public libraries, where children are allowed to take home books to share and return, builds bridges between home and school activities. In a borrow-a-book program, children should be allowed to sign out at least two books, one for the child to read to the parents and one for the parents to read to the child.

Principals can value these relationships centered on learning by ensuring the visitors are welcome and the school climate is inviting for parents. The principal values these relationships by being visible and present at these events and by knowing and celebrating the children and their work.

EARLY IDENTIFICATION PROCESSES

Establishing processes in school that identify the need for more intentional literacy instruction is key to providing appropriate intervention. The school team, including administrator, resource teachers, and classroom teachers, can establish processes for meeting in the first few months of school to share and discuss the observations and assessment the teacher has made. Through early identification, specific needs can be determined and plans made for additional support and family contact. It is important to develop regular communication plans with parents and to include them in developing and delivering literacy programs.

Early Intervention Programs

It is important to have plans in place that allow teachers and schools to respond quickly and effectively by increasing the time and intensity of literacy instruction for children who come to school without much experience.

The kindergarten and Grade 1 teachers have developed a reading program that is run by classroom volunteers. Children who will benefit from additional reading time each day are given this opportunity early in the school year. Volunteers are trained to teach reading strategies (basic concepts of print, using pictures for clues, finding familiar words, using first and last sounds). Some of the volunteers are high school students on co-op programs, and others are parents. The teachers ask parents of children whose skills are less developed to be involved in the training and those that can participate by reading in class and at home with their children. Sequential lessons, with books of increasing difficulty, are carefully chosen to ensure children and volunteers experience early and ongoing success.

The resource teachers, who work closely with classroom teachers, monitor and provide more specific interventions for students who appear to have specific learning difficulties.

When school leaders support, nurture, and feed the relationship between home and school, children grow and their literacy skills flourish.

CHAPTER SUMMARY

In this chapter, the focus has been on providing the school leader and learning team with standards complete with examples, to review the school culture and the current construction of the early literacy environment. Questions have been provided to guide this assessment. Ideally this work is done with an improvement team made up of a combination of administration and staff. School leaders will work with staff to determine the evidence that addresses each question and what that evidence conveys to students, parents, and colleagues. Part of this assessment will be to determine steps to be taken toward an action plan for improvement in creating rich literacy environments along the continuum of improvement toward excellence.

QUESTIONS FOR DISCUSSION

- What do we demonstrate through our actions about our current beliefs about young children as learners? And about the ability of children who come from diverse backgrounds?
- Are programs designed to be flexible to differences in children's learning styles and to diverse levels of learning?
- What messages do the literacy programs we have created convey to children who come from less literate homes?
- How do our beliefs play out in our planning and communication among ourselves, with children, and with parents?
- What dispositions are being developed in our classrooms and through our programs?
- Which aspects of the six Ts for exemplary teaching—time, text, teaching, talk, tasks, and testing—are our strengths, and which are our weaknesses?
- How might multiage buddies be utilized to enrich literacy programs to provide a more inclusive environment?
- What input do children have into their course of study?
- What is the role of teacher—instructor and co-constructor of knowledge?
- What role does inquiry play in the design of lessons and units of study?
- Is the classroom organized to teach and support children's learning?
- How is children's work documented and shared with children and their parents?

- How prevalent is talk, projects and investigations, stories, and storytelling?
- What forms of literacy are evident in the classroom?
- What involvement do parents have in their child's education?
- What is the process for identification and intervention for learning difficulties?
- What do we do when children do not appear to be benefiting from the school environment?

CHAPTER 3

Instructional
Leadership

The Tools You Will Need

To be effective instructional leaders, school leaders have to have the appropriate tools to review early literacy programs, to refine school practices, to select the best teachers, to provide professional development, and to renew programs toward meaningful change.

This chapter addresses the big questions: What are worthy literacy goals? What are the essential literacy learnings or key expectations? How will we assess literacy learning? What counts as evidence? When I visit classrooms, what do I look for? In this chapter, the ideas presented in Chapter 2 are translated into practical tools and processes that principals can use with teachers and teaching teams in the area of curriculum development.

DEVELOPING A VISION:
CHANGING CULTURES

The first step to any change is having a vision as a desired outcome that inspires and energizes others to achieve a target or goal. The school leader has to develop this vision with staff of where the school is headed or what any new practice looks like.

On a trip to Scandinavia, I visited a community where I was struck by the vision that founded the following posted mission statement: "We will be known by how we treat our children." Not merely words, we saw this translated into practice when we visited a housing construction site where the first thing being built was a playground to ensure the children had something to do and to keep them safe. There was certainly no doubt in my mind that people in this community understood the vision and took action to ensure they were achieving this outcome.

Once the school leader has developed a vision, the next step is to determine the gaps between current practice (where are we now?) and future goals (where do we want to be?). The following chart presents an overview of how programs for young children have evolved and gives some positive future direction to assist school leaders with developing this vision. The chart can be used with teaching teams as a starting point for identifying the next steps for improving the early literacy programs in their own schools. Principals can also use the chart with teachers to perform a gap analysis on their own practices. Note: The chart can be found in the "Tools for School Leaders" at the back of the book as a reproducible checklist (Tool 2).

Assessing the Gaps in Literacy Programs

	Then	Now	Ahead
Curriculum Design	❑ TAUGHT curriculum ❑ Teacher INSTRUCTION ❑ Teacher as expert ❑ Whole-group instruction ❑ Teacher-designed activities	❑ LEARNED curriculum ❑ Teacher INSTRUCTION with teacher-designed activities ❑ Child as learner ❑ Whole and small group lessons ❑ Some student choices	❑ NEGOTIATED curriculum ❑ Student CONSTRUCTION of knowledge in collaboration with teacher ❑ Child and teacher as learners ❑ Individual and group contributions to projects and investigations

	Then	*Now*	*Ahead*
Instruction	❑ Teacher dominates ❑ Whole group instruction ❑ Teacher-designed activities	❑ Whole and small group lessons organized by the teacher ❑ Some student choices in teacher-designed activities	❑ Individual and group contributions to lessons and ongoing projects and investigations
Goals	❑ Socialization goals ❑ Reading as a goal	❑ Literacy and numeracy goals (phonemes, reading strategies)	❑ Integrated understandings of literacy (across the curriculum)
Assessment	❑ Teacher as assessor ❑ Local curriculum	❑ Standard curriculum ❑ External standards	❑ Collaborative and self-assessment on continuums of learning (standards based)
Discipline	❑ Discipline by fear	❑ Discipline by choice	❑ Discipline by design

GUIDING PRINCIPLES

The principal will want to establish guiding principles for literacy programs with the school's leadership team and the early years teaching team (teachers, assistants, parents) in order to lay the groundwork for the school's early literacy program and provide a foundation to keep it firmly grounded. These guiding principles are agreed-upon assumptions that will guide future decision making.

Principals can start a conversation with teams about how children learn and the key components of an effective literacy program by presenting the following statements for discussion:

- Children have tremendous potential.
- Children are naturally curious about how the world works.

- Children are in the process of constructing their own knowledge about how the world works.
- The teacher must first seek to understand the child.
- Teachers are observers, challengers, and provokers of ideas.
- Teachers are partners in learning; teachers are researchers and co-investigators.
- Learning can be assessed through observation and recording.

The resource list provided at the back of the book references readings and Web sites that can support these discussions. Teachers can take a reading, summarize it, and bring it to the group for sharing of key points. Once teachers have researched and discussed high-quality practices, have them come together to formulate guiding principles for the school's early literacy program. The following sentence starters can be used with teams for developing guiding principles for your school:

1. All children learn when . . .

2. Young children learn best by . . .

3. The teacher's role is to . . .

4. Programs will be individualized by . . .

5. Learning will be assessed through . . .

6. Parents can participate by . . .

Having developed teachers' awareness, the school leader may want to develop a plan for professional staff development with teachers, offering professional readings, access to consultants, examples of exemplary practice, visits to model classrooms, and other resources prior to beginning or refining implementation.

DEFINING LITERACY: THREE KEY EXPECTATIONS

It is critical for the school leader to have a clear purpose and expectations for the early literacy program in order to direct positive change. Too often, literacy in our culture, interpreted by schools for the purpose of educating the young, is most commonly defined as the ability to read and write and to comprehend what we read, a functional literacy at best. Is it not far more important to develop the skills and habits of mind required to proficiently communicate in the literacies of the culture in the terms of mathematics, technology, science, language, and the arts? When it comes to literacy learning, a balanced early childhood curriculum aims for (a) social-emotional development, (b) intellectual development, and (c) the acquisition of meaningful and useful skills (Katz, 1999).

The key expectations for balanced early literacy that follow have been developed around these three suggested outcomes to guide teachers and principals in this work. Note: This list can also be found in the "Tools for School Leaders" at the back of the book as a reproducible checklist (Tool 3).

Key Literacy Expectations

(a) Social-Emotional/Affective Development

Through interaction with texts and stories, as well as interactions with others through sharing, role-playing, cooperative learning, and large-group simulation, young children will be encouraged to dialogue, critique, compare, negotiate, hypothesize, and problem solve. Multiple perspectives promote both a sense of group membership and the uniqueness of self.

The following expectations outline the key expectations for literacy in the area of social-emotional/affective development:

- Learn social conventions (taking turns, tone of voice, eye contact, acknowledging another's ideas)
- Recognize and develop empathy related to feelings and mood
- Learn moral and ethical lessons
- Take on various roles (develop perspective, make personal connections)
- Develop an awareness of cultural similarities and differences

(b) Intellectual Development

Through thinking about stories and information provided through texts, young children will learn to think beyond the literal to the inferred and to question and critique ideas, texts, and perspectives.

The following expectations more specifically outline the key expectations for literacy in the area of intellectual development:

- Make sense of experience, seeking explanations
- Theorize about cause and effect
- Make predictions
- Hypothesize about observations
- Analyze and synthesize information
- Develop personal connections and express feeling responses

(c) Development of Useful and Meaningful Skills

Through engagement in the various disciplines, young children will learn to listen and respond, using the languages and literacies that are characteristic of the various disciplines of language, mathematics, science, technology, and the arts. The key expectations have been categorized using the multiple intelligences headings.

The following expectations more specifically outline the key expectations for literacy in the area of developing useful and meaningful skills.

Linguistic

- Tell, dictate, and dramatize personal, cultural, and invented stories
- Read and retell stories from books, demonstrating concepts of print (left to right, front to back)
- Understand symbols and begin to make connections between sounds and symbols, symbols and meanings (letter names and sounds, phonemes, rhyme, letter recognition and formation, word families, invented spellings)
- Experiment with words, word sounds, word order, and meanings, incorporating new vocabulary, meanings, and rules of speech
- Show that words are units of meaning (read and write names, environmental signs)
- Experiment with expression and representation of ideas and feelings using movement, dance, talk, writing, drawing, story forms, paint, music, dramatic play, symbols (numbers, gestures, pictures), and so forth
- Listen and interpret play, talk, pictures, story, symbol, and print
- Ask questions about facts, the physical world, and relationships
- Observe real-life settings where reading and writing are used

Logical-Mathematical

- Develop and use mathematical language and symbols related to quantity, size, shape, pattern, and relationships
- Use specific language to explain procedures
- Sort, classify and order, name, and describe the categories and relationships
- Identify problems and use strategies for solving problems (asking questions, posing problems, collecting and recording information, identifying patterns, determining outcomes)
- Use senses to observe and make discoveries
- Predict events based on observations

Spatial/Visual

- Use media (rigid and fluid) to communicate stories, ideas, and experiences
- Develop a visual vocabulary related to line, texture, color, shape, space, and pattern
- Make personal connections to works of art (including art, music, live performance, dance, film, and video) and develop personal responses
- Demonstrate an understanding of visual media as a language (predict next action, illustrate stories)

Musical/Rhythmic

- Develop and use music vocabulary related to beat, tone, and so forth
- Respond to music through movement, art, poetry, and sound
- Create rhythm, beat, rhyme, and soundscapes

Bodily-Kinesthetic

- Develop and use vocabulary related to movement
- Manipulate tools and instruments with purpose and control
- Express ideas, issues, and emotions through dance/movement
- Recall and re-create using materials (dramatic play)

Interpersonal and Intrapersonal

- Communicate feelings and ideas
- Act as a member of a community, negotiating, sharing, and caring
- Explore new roles: imaginings, feelings, and attitudes

ASSESSING LEARNING: WHAT COUNTS AS EVIDENCE?

The allure to quantify almost everything has educators busy examining what the child knows compared to others or grade standards (e.g., how many letters and sounds a child knows) and missing the child's understanding or construction of knowledge and the qualities that characterize a particular child's thinking. What we typically think of as hard evidence, the numbers and statistics, tells very little about what children know or are able to do, what they are thinking or how they are constructing their understanding of the world in which they live.

What provides the most information about children's learning are samples of their thinking presented along continuums of learning (conceptual, thinking, and representational). These include samples of children's work and teachers' documentation of children's thinking over time.

Principals will want to encourage and support finding spaces and methods for celebrating children's work in public ways.

The following are some examples:

- Photo displays
- Portfolios
- Performances
- Newsletters
- Newspaper reports
- Showcases
- Culminating activities
- Literacy events

Providing time for teachers to meet and discuss children's work based on the literacy expectations is important.

MANAGEMENT BY WALKING AROUND AND WHAT TO LOOK FOR

It is often useful for the school principal to have a checklist of things to look for when visiting classrooms, talking to teachers, and designing programs. The following table provides an at-a-glance record of some of the things to look and listen for when assessing "where are we now?" and "where do we want to go?" Sharing this with teachers is a good starting point for discussion about programs, leading to program review and plans for improvement.

Principals can use the following chart in a number of ways:

1. As criteria for classroom observations to assist principals in knowing what a good literacy program looks like

2. As a management-by-walking-around checklist—a record of what principals see when visiting classrooms

3. As reflective questions—a starting point for discussion with teachers about ways they might develop their programs

4. As teacher performance reviews—to provide possible categories for the collection of evidence (e.g., environment, timetables, units of study). Based on the evidence, principals can assist teachers with determining professional learning goals.

Note: The chart can also be found in the "Tools for School Leaders" at the back of the book as a reproducible checklist (Tool 4).

Checklist for Walk-Throughs

	A Good Early Literacy Program IS	*A Good Early Literacy Program IS NOT*
Classroom Environment	❑ Language-rich environment (talk, talk, talk, print, print, print in context) ❑ Student engagement ❑ Student questions	❑ Dittos ❑ Teacher-directed circles (30 minutes) ❑ Teacher talk dominates

(Continued)

(Continued)

	A Good Early Literacy Program IS	A Good Early Literacy Program IS NOT
Timetables	❑ Large blocks of time for self-directed activity/play	❑ Short activity sessions and large blocks of time for instruction
Units of Study	❑ Meaningful topics of study ❑ Designed around BIG ideas large enough for diversity of ideas and inclusion ❑ Negotiated between children's ideas/interests and teacher's knowledge of children's interests ❑ Story-based units of study based on binary opposites ❑ Focused on the dispositions of learning ❑ Authentic links to the natural and real world ❑ Apprenticeships	❑ Small ideas of little consequence (story character such as *Clifford the Big Red Dog*, the color red)
Projects	❑ Emerge from children's ideas and interests: shadows, puddles, tall buildings, construction sites, nature, etc. ❑ Develop over time. Sufficient time is dedicated to the project to allow discussion of new ideas, negotiation, conflicts, revisiting ideas, note progress, and to see movement of ideas ❑ Concrete, personal from real experiences, important to children, should be large enough for diversity of ideas ❑ Rich in interpretive and representational expression ❑ Multiple means of representing and communicating meaning ❑ Stimulates activity and discussion	❑ Decided and designed by the teacher ❑ Narrow focus ❑ Single outcomes ❑ Little choice for students ❑ Paper-pencil focus ❑ Little meaning ❑ Engages only a few "good" children ❑ Quiet

	A Good Early Literacy Program IS	A Good Early Literacy Program IS NOT
Resources and Materials	❏ Rich materials designed to elicit the languages of science, social studies, music, dance, drama, and mathematics ❏ Rich in interpretive and representational expression ❏ Media include paint, modeling clay, rich texture materials, building and construction materials (tiles, wood, blocks), dramatic materials (scarves, baskets, streamers), science materials (sand, water) ❏ Manipulatives such as things that pour, float, etc.	❏ Dittos, flashcards ❏ One-dimensional materials (number cards) ❏ One- and two-dimensional qualities ❏ Limited potential and appeal for children ❏ Traditional teaching materials (letters and numbers)
Teaching Strategies	❏ Teachers prepare the environment for active exploration and interaction ❏ Teachers work alongside children to facilitate their involvement by asking questions, offering suggestions, adding more complex materials or ideas to a situation ❏ Teachers accept children's ideas and use them in their planning ❏ Teachers scaffold ideas of the children	❏ Teacher directed and teacher designed ❏ Teacher talk dominates ❏ Irrelevant to children and their interests
Media Representation	❏ Multiple, creative, constructive ❏ Opportunities for exploration: What is this material? What does it do? What can I do with the material?	❏ One- and two-dimensional ❏ Single purposed ❏ Primary colors ❏ Only used at particular times and for particular reasons

(Continued)

(Continued)

	A Good Early Literacy Program IS	A Good Early Literacy Program IS NOT
	❑ Variation in color, texture, pattern: help children see the colors, tones, hues; help children feel the texture, the similarities and differences ❑ Presented in an artistic manner, it too should be aesthetically pleasing to look at it, should invite you to touch, admire, inspire ❑ Revisited throughout many projects to help children see the possibilities	❑ Teacher directed
Circles and Meetings	❑ Short meetings of 10 minutes ❑ Small group, guided and shared reading ❑ Small group games	❑ Longer than 10–15 minutes ❑ Children are expected to sit, watch, be quiet, listen ❑ Teacher dominates, talking to the whole group, and telling children what to do ❑ Teacher questions focus on low-level thinking
Assessment	❑ Teachers record children's learning and progress through visual representations of their ideas ❑ Photos, anecdotal descriptions, children's work, video and audio recordings, performances, events, projects, questions, experiments, three-dimensional structures	❑ Single-page tests ❑ Focused on letters, sounds, numbers

	A Good Early Literacy Program IS	*A Good Early Literacy Program* IS NOT
Language and Literacy Development	❑ Opportunities to see how reading and writing are useful, modeled by people who use these skills to communicate ❑ Authentic and meaningful experiences with language and literacy: listening to and reading stories and poems; taking field trips; dictating ideas, stories, and signs; seeing print in use; participating in dramatic play and other experiences requiring communication; talking informally with people; experimenting with writing by drawing, copying, and inventing their own spelling	❑ Isolated skills such as single letters, reciting the alphabet, singing the ABC song, letter sounds, coloring, forming letters and numbers

What Does Balanced Literacy Look Like in the Early Years?

The following list provides a more detailed look specifically at the concept of balanced literacy, developing specific criteria for the early years. Note: It can also be found as a reproducible checklist in the "Tools for School Leaders" at the back of the book (Tool 5).

Meetings and Circle Times

- Brief and to the point (10 minutes)
- Meet in small groups, ideally five children

- Initiate thinking and activity through challenges, materials, and so forth
- Review, reflect, and share children's work and ideas

Read-Alouds: Daily and Frequent

- During circle times, to prompt children's thinking
- Following project times to sum up, to advance children's thinking
- During project times (with an individual or small group), from a self-selected book to address a child's or children's question (read by a volunteer specific to an area such as the classroom library)
- During sharing/reflection time, from a child's dictation for dramatization or to share an investigation

Shared Reading

- At arrival, children self-select books and read them in pairs, small groups, or on their own.
- During project times, books and print material are available for children to read together in small groups to advance their thinking and answer their questions.
- During sharing/reflection time, teachers and children read from dictated text.

Individual Reading

- At arrival, children self-select books and read them in pairs, small groups, or on their own.
- Read-aloud books stay in the classroom library for children to read on their own.
- Children read signs and organize materials according to signs and labels.

Modeled Writing

- Teachers record children's dictation.
- Teachers create environmental signs conveying messages for children to decode (closed, open, exit, entrance, stop, go) and sign-up sheets for centers, projects, turns, and so forth.

Shared Writing

- Children create their own messages with the teacher's help.

Individual Writing

- Children sign in each morning (record name on a chart).
- Children sign in to interest centers.
- Representational writing including recorded math work, for example, patterns by one, two, or three dimensions.

The following examples provide concrete ideas for principals of what reading and writing might look like in early years classrooms.

Reading Examples

Three children sit in the middle of a construction site they have created with big blocks and examine the construction signs in a picture book. They decide which signs they will make for their site. One child reads the word danger *and another thinks he knows which word says,* keep out.

In another area of the room, children lie on bellies, reading a map of the town. They point out roads and try to determine where they live. They come up with the idea of building their own town and making a map of it.

Writing Examples

Each morning children sign in on a sheet of paper attached to a clipboard. The teacher tells them that this is the record of attendance, and children get an opportunity to practice printing their name for a particular purpose.

The children are having difficulty getting the fountain in the washroom to turn off and on. At their class meeting, they decide to write a note to leave on the fountain for the custodian to read when cleaning the room at the end of the day. Together with a classroom aide, they compose the note "bokn" and tape it above the fountain. The next day, a few rush into the washroom to see the result. A sign above the fountain simply states "fixed."

PLANNING MODELS

Critical to the development of a good unit of study for young children is the selection of an authentic topic worthy of study, one that will be meaningful to children and capture their interest. Considering the range of possible topics for study in school, this task is a difficult one, and teachers have to be selective. Not all topics are equally promising in terms of their educational potential. Principals can assist teachers, right from the start, by guiding them to choose topics with the greatest learning potential. We start, at the beginning, with an exercise to determine what makes a topic worthy of study.

1. Topics for Study: The Big Ideas

School leaders might use an exercise such as the following:

1. Have teachers take the list of topics provided.

2. Have teachers apply the criteria of "What makes a worthy study?" to each topic.

3. Ask teachers to put the topics in order from those that have the greatest learning potential to those that have the least learning potential.

Food groups

Blue

Valentine's Day

Garden

Fairy tales

Conflict

Clifford the Big Red Dog

Animals

Going shopping

The senses

Puddles

Teddy bears

Dinosaurs

Archaeology

Shadows

Roads

Brave/cowardly

Study Criteria: What Makes a Worthy Study in the Early Years?

- Does it engage and interest children?
- Does it lend itself to the study of issues and opposites?
- Does it promote a disposition of reading, writing, and critical thinking?
- Does it enable children to understand the value of literary and numeracy in real life contexts?
- Does it offer ideas for dramatic play and representation?
- Does it encourage children to ask questions and seek sources of information outside of school?
- Is it likely to sustain interest over time?
- Does it facilitate communication with parents, particularly around children's learning?

Once teachers have gone through a process such as this, they should become more selective in their studies.

2. Unit and Lesson Planning

In this section, five planning strategies are outlined from simple to complex. The idea is to take teachers from surface-level planning to deeper levels of thinking when planning studies with and for young children. School leaders may use these five strategies—challenges, projects, mythic planning framework, multiple intelligences planning framework, and integrated planning framework—as examples for teachers, to encourage teachers to try some of these strategies in their planning, and to set goals for working toward more complex forms of planning.

(a) Challenges

Challenges are open-ended problems that direct and engage children for part of a day as a lesson to begin or further a topic or unit of study.

Challenges are a great place to start exploring planning strategies with teachers. They are an easy and reinforcing strategy for teachers to use since young children respond readily to challenges that can be put to them verbally or in writing. They can be used at the beginning of a circle to stimulate conversation, at the end of a circle to direct project activities, in the gym for creative movement, or during a story to provoke response. Make sure challenges are open-ended to stimulate thinking, entice creative and multiple responses, and provide for personal connections.

Examples of Challenges

Ask children to

- Build the tallest tower
- Move like a butterfly
- Use parts of the story in your play
- Solve the mystery of the most dangerous dinosaur
- Imagine that a character from the story comes to our room

(b) Projects

Projects are in-depth investigations of real world topics, each lasting a week, month, or year. Principals can use this framework to develop authentic studies with teachers who are committed to going deeper in their planning. This framework works especially well when teachers start by building on real events that are already part of their classroom experience, for example, shopping at the grocery store or visiting a pizza parlor.

By definition, a project is an in-depth investigation of a real world topic worthy of children's attention and effort.

Projects are in-depth studies of concepts, ideas, and interests that arise from the interests of the group or the environment.

Considered an adventure, projects may last one week or could continue throughout the school year. Throughout a project, teachers help children make decisions about the direction of study, the ways in which the group will research the topic, the representational medium that will demonstrate and showcase the topic, and the selection of materials needed to represent the work. Note: The following can be found as a reproducible checklist in the "Tools for School Leaders" at the back of the book (Tool 6).

Criteria for a Good Project

- A project emerges from children's ideas and interests
- The teacher knows the interest to children (e.g., can introduce a project: shadows, puddles, tall buildings, construction sites, nature, etc.)
- A project is long enough to develop over time, to incorporate new ideas, to allow negotiation, to provoke conflict of ideas, so that ideas can be revisited, and so that progress of ideas is evident
- A project is often concrete, comes from real experiences, is important to children, is broad enough to allow for a diversity of ideas and rich in its potential for interpretive/representational expression

Steps in Developing a Project

Teacher planning:

- Brainstorm and create a web of ideas from a topic.
- Outline important events.
- Look into sites, sources, and experts to further the study and put it into a real-world context.
- Collect resources.

Step 1: Planning With Students

- Stimulate the children's interest in the topic through a story, video, or object.
- Collect ideas and map out what children already know.
- List questions children would like to investigate/answer.

Step 2: Project Work

- Discuss and record what questions they have, whom they might talk to, and what they might bring to the classroom. Discuss what they are likely to see and do.
- On trips, take field notes and make sketches and decide what they would like to learn more about.
- People with firsthand experience of the topics through their work or travel may come to visit and talk with children, respond to questions, and engage in discussion.
- Discuss trips; re-create accounts of what happened, whom they talked with, what they saw, and what they learned. Sketches can become the basis for drawings, paintings, and construction of models; information books are consulted; new questions are raised and letters written. Plan follow-up activities.

Step 3: Culminating Event/Celebration of Learning

- Showcase the children's work to other children, parents, and staff through a display, a performance, or an event.
- Children personalize the new knowledge by presenting it through imaginative stories and dramatic sequences.

Adapted from Sylvia Chard's (2001) work on *The Project Approach in Early Childhood and Elementary Education.* For more examples, visit www.projectapproach.org.

(c) Mythic Planning Framework

Mythic planning framework is a story framework that allows teachers to take content and structure it around a story framework or as a way for children to explore central story issues (e.g., love/hate). It can be used in a single lesson, for structuring dramatic responses to a story, or as a unit of study.

Principals can introduce the mythic planning framework in a variety of ways, including as a response to a story or developed into a unit of study. It uses a story or narrative frame for planning. Teachers must start with a central story issue, one that engages children's imaginations, works through conflict created by the opposing forces, and resolves the conflict in the end. Young children are especially responsive to this structure because this is how they think. Almost any topic or problem can be transformed into a story, where children as the players act out the roles and take the conflict to conclusion.

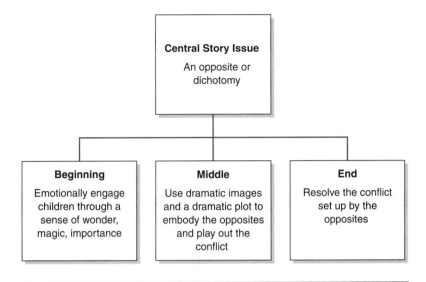

Adapted from Egan (1997). For examples of Egan's work on imaginative education and mythic planning from the Imaginative Education Research Group, go to www.ierg.net/teaching/plan-frameworks/index.html.

Example Using the Mythic Planning Framework

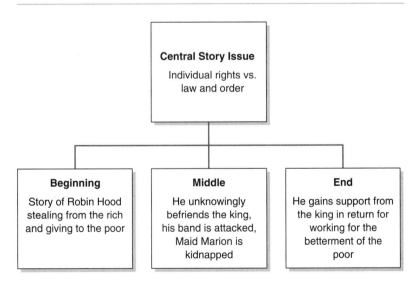

Note: This template can be found in the "Tools for School Leaders" at the back of the book (Tool 7).

(d) Multiple Intelligences Planning Framework

The multiple intelligences framework allows teachers to plan so that children can explore topics using their preferred styles of learning. It ensures all styles of learning are addressed.

As an introductory level, principals can present the multiple intelligences through this planning framework for teachers who are not familiar with it or who do not use it in their planning.

The multiple intelligence planning framework is one way to ensure that children are being exposed to literacy through multiple means and in multiple forms. Using the web and chart provided, teachers can plot out the activities in which students will be engaged at different centers in the room or through different key events through a unit. A big idea or topic is placed at the center with the activities positioned around it. The chart outlines some activities and materials that apply. Teachers can use the chart for ideas on what to include at each center or for key activities that match each intelligence. An example of a theme-based study is provided.

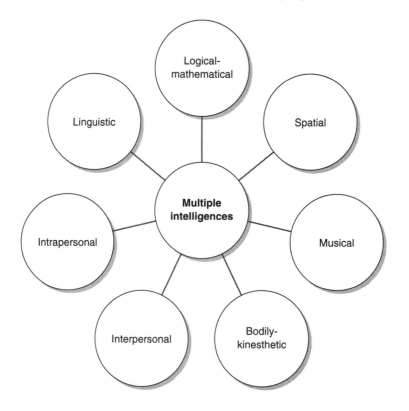

At a more advanced level, principals can use the multiple intelligence framework to take planning to a deeper level by delving with teachers into what it means to think as a mathematician and how that is promoted through activities and materials in the classroom. The question is posed in the middle, and mathematical thinking is developed through the various centers. Note: This template can be found in the "Tools for School Leaders" at the back of the book (Tool 8).

Chart: Tapping Into Seven Learning Styles Using the Multiple Intelligences in Planning

Children Who Are Highly	Think	Activities	Materials
Linguistic	In words, letters, and sounds, stories	Reading, listening, writing, telling, and acting out stories and poems, playing word games and rhymes, reading for information and answers, discussing ideas, arguing points of view	Picture books from different genres, tapes, writing tools (colored pencils, markers, crayons), paper, small books (diaries, scrapbooks), computers, acting out points of view, small theaters, puppets, familiar stories, popular stories and fairy tales, visits to the library
Logical-mathematical	By reasoning what makes sense, and what is next	Experimenting, questioning, figuring out logical puzzles, calculating, etc.	Things to explore and think about (rocks, earth, plants, stones, small creatures), science materials (sand, water, sieves, graduated cylinders, flashlights, mirrors, thermometers, and scales), math manipulatives (building blocks, gears, puzzles, items to sort and categorize), calculators, computers, trips to the planetarium, science museum, etc.

(Continued)

(Continued)

Children Who Are Highly	Think	Activities	Materials
Spatial	In images and pictures	Designing, doodling, drawing, visualizing	Art and architecture books, designs, diagrams of cross sections of buildings and machines, art materials (paint, water, inks, clay, fabrics, feathers, sequins, yarn), and building materials (LEGO, blocks), visual media (video, camera, movies, slides, photos), imagination games, mazes, optical illusions, trips to art museums, etc.
Bodily-kinesthetic	Through somatic sensations	Dancing, running, jumping, building, touching, gesturing, etc.	Books about the body, athletes, anatomy, posters showing sequences of movements, role-play props (scarves, hats), movement materials (streamers, balloons), things to build (models), sports and physical games, tactile and sensory experiences
Musical	Via rhythms and melodies	Singing, whistling, humming, tapping feet and hands, listening, etc.	Song books and books about songs, rhythm, pattern and sound books, sing-along recordings, CDs, video recordings, earphones, musical instruments (piano, drums), posters of instruments and composers, musical scores and notations, staff paper, trips to concerts, etc.

Children Who Are Highly	Think	Activities	Materials
Interpersonal	By bouncing ideas off other people	Leading, organizing, relating, manipulating, mediating, etc.	Books about relationships, friendships, culture and diversity, ethnic foods and traditions, telephones, puppets, role-play props, brainstorming, friends, group games for two or three, social gatherings, community events, clubs, buddy reading, intergenerational activities, apprenticeships, etc.
Intrapersonal	Deeply inside themselves	Setting goals, mediating, dreaming, being quiet, planning, etc.	Books about wishes, dreams, emotions, poetry, big questions, secret places, time alone, self-paced projects, choices, journals, diaries, portfolios, audio recordings, etc.

Source: Adapted with permission from "Multiple Intelligences in the Classroom" (p. 27), by Thomas Armstrong–Alexandria, VA: ASCD. © 1994 by ASCD. Used with permission. Learn more about ASCD at www.ascd.org.

(e) Integrated Planning Framework: Using the Dispositions for Learning

The integrated planning framework integrates the project, mythic, and multiple intelligences. This is most practical as a unit of study.

The integrated planning framework is the most complex of the models provided. Principals will want to introduce it to teachers who are already integrating their planning, have a tendency to use real life experiences in their planning, or have worked through some of the other models and are up for the challenge.

Example Using the Multiple Intelligence Framework

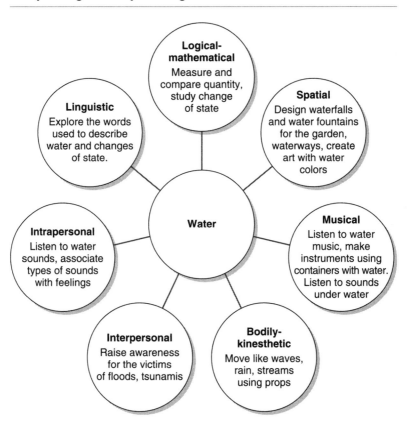

Early years and kindergarten-age learners are readily engaged in the literacies of science and social studies (inquiry), math (problem solving), and language and arts (communication) when the focus of their study shifts from information to a study in how people engaged in various professions think. They love to role-play, and when they are challenged with problems that demand particular kinds of thinking, they are instantly engaged.

The chart on page 93 illustrates how each discipline is linked to particular ways of thinking. It provides roles that children can take on to portray this thinking and the type of literacy that children can be engaged in during their role play. Note: This template can be found in the "Tools for School Leaders" at the back of the book (Tool 9).

Discipline	Habits of Mind or Dispositions	Roles Children Take On	Literacy
Science	Inquiry model: Asking questions, developing hypothesis, collecting information, analyzing data, drawing conclusions	Archaeologist Paleontologist Doctor Scientist Investigator Detective Police Officer	Experiments, lab reports, diagrams
History/social studies	Recording and documenting events: dating, labeling, storing	Archivist Curator Historian	Timelines, stories, historical records, plays, artifacts
Mathematics	Measuring and quantifying, classifying and sorting, finding patterns, understanding relationships, developing formulas	Accountant Statistician Architect	Graphs, tables, drawings, numbers, calculations, inventions, formulas, logic problems
Language	Communicating meaning: developing thesis, argument or idea, catching the reader's attention, developing plausibility, stringing a tale, implied meanings	Reporter Novelist Politician Speech writer Lawyer	Narratives, tall tales, reports
Art/spatial	Interpreting	Musician Artist Architect Mechanic Dancer Actor	Paintings, drawings, drafts, labels, plays

The next section takes the study of dinosaurs, a traditional unit of study in the kindergarten classroom, and reconceptualizes it for a more deeply integrated and inclusive study that taps into the dispositions of learning and engages students through story and myth. Principals can share this example with teachers to demonstrate how some of their traditional units can be transformed from a focus on facts to a focus on thinking.

RECONCEPTUALIZING TRADITIONAL UNIT PLANS

A typical unit found in many early years classrooms is the study of dinosaurs because these creatures fascinate so many young learners, especially some of the boys. Dinosaurs captivate young children's imaginations because of their fantastic appearance, their dominant size, and complicated names. Traditionally this unit of study might include such things as reading books about dinosaurs at the reading center and during circle time, measuring dinosaur replicas at the math center, playing with dinosaurs at the sand center, and perhaps dramatizing with dinosaur costumes at the dramatic play center.

Example of a Traditional Planning Scheme: Unit on Dinosaurs

Blocks: Building the badlands	**Paint:** Painting a mural of dinosaur land	**Books:** Books about dinosaurs
Drama: Dinosaur costumes	**Arts & crafts:** Making dinosaurs and reptiles from egg cartons	**Manipulatives:** Dinosaur puzzles
Science: Study of eggs, reptiles, bones	**Clay:** Sculpting dinosaur replicas	**Computer:** Dinosaur games
Sand/water: Miniature dinosaur models in a dinosaur land		**Pets:** Reptiles

What would happen if teachers were to reconceptualize this study, from its rather narrow focus on facts and information into a study that engages student in a particular way of thinking? What would that look like?

We begin by asking, "What is the intellectual discipline or the principled thought that underlies the study of dinosaurs?" The study of dinosaurs falls within the discipline of science and is carried out by paleontologists, the scientists who engage in the scientific study of dinosaurs and demonstrate the habits of mind or disciplines required for this study.

So next we ask, "What are the rules that guide this scientific inquiry?" To develop this unit in more meaningful ways, we have to examine the thinking of scientists as they go about uncovering these puzzles of the past. Using tools of inquiry, they ask questions, gather evidence, and pose hypotheses and test them based on current knowledge and additional evidence. In developing the unit of study, the teacher asks, "What is the overarching problem to be solved?" In this example, the teacher uses the big idea of "Uncovering Puzzles From the Past" to challenge the children. The activities and lessons are transformed to encourage students to ask questions, uncover clues, piece together puzzles, and solve mysteries.

Example of Children Engaged in Solving a Dinosaur Puzzle

Mitchell surveys the pile of bones in front of him, "Now where did I put the Tyrannosaur head?"

Donnie offers to help, "There it is, Mitchell."

"Where?" Mitchell asks. Finding the piece, he rejects it: "No, that is not the one." He offers Donnie another clue to help in the search. "The one with the up and down teeth."

Mitchell picks up the two identical pieces, turns one and places them together so they match, "Hey two heads . . ." [He makes a roaring sound].

Donnie draws a backbone piece toward him. "Hey, let's both do Tyrannosaurus."

"Wait a sec," Mitchell pauses.

The teacher finds and places two identical pieces on the table between the boys. "I think you have two dinosaurs here," she suggests.

"Yeah!" Mitchell exclaims. "You can do this one and I will do the Tyrannosaurus." Then he finds another headpiece like the one he has. "See, there is another head."

"Huh?" says Danny, acting surprised.

"Now we can both do . . . Tyrannosaurus," exclaims Mitchell.

This example shows two kindergarten-age boys attempting to make sense of the pile of puzzle pieces on the table in front of them. It demonstrates the potential for inquiry when children are given the problem of trying to figure out what kind of dinosaurs are in the pieces before them; they naturally engage in scientific thinking by asking questions, posing hypotheses, verifying their thinking with evidence, and drawing conclusions (Geddis, Lynch, & Speir, 1998).

The teacher's role is to transform the subject matter in order to bridge the gap between the teacher's understanding and the student's. The teacher does this by identifying and understanding the problems students are trying to solve, the differences in children's thinking, and the rules students are using to solve their own problems. As a mutual participant, the teacher provides wait time so students can formulate their own ideas, rephrases to clarify thinking, asks questions to focus problem solving, gives reasons, reinforces contributions, and is a watchful listener who is looking for moments to engage with germinating ideas. As Bamberger (1991) noted, the teacher acknowledges and explores the ideas that the children present and stops their action to probe their thinking, clarify and confirm their ideas, and take advantage of the opportunity to extend their thinking.

Example of the New Unit: Uncovering Puzzles From the Past

The following example shows how a teacher might rework a dinosaur unit to engage the children in scientific inquiry through role play and what this new unit might look like. The disposition column outlines the different roles children will be playing and the kinds of thinking they will be engaged in for these roles. The investigation column displays the kinds of activities they will be engaged in, and the representation column shows the ways they will be recording their work. School leaders can share this planning sheet with teachers to assist them in their planning. Note: This template can be found in the "Tools for School Leaders" at the back of the book (Tool 10).

Disposition	Investigation	Representation
Scientist (inquiry model): asking questions, developing hypotheses, collecting information, analyzing data, drawing conclusion **Museum curator:** recording and documenting events: dating, labeling, storing, showcasing **Reporter:** Preparing invitations, media releases, stories	Finding and solving puzzles Measuring Classifying and sorting Comparing found materials to reference materials Identifying artifacts Sharing information Showcasing finds Hosting visits	Diagrams Photos Labels Displays Dioramas

This new study is not limited to dinosaurs but broadened to encompass different artifacts from the past, and because this topic is more inclusive, it includes those girls who would likely opt out of a study of dinosaurs.

A story element is added and the conflict between the opposites of living/extinct or lost/found is developed by having the children listen to and tell tales of lost treasure and exploring the idea of lost civilizations such as Atlantis and the Egyptian pyramids with their buried treasures. Family stories might also be included so children can discover what these tell us about different historical time and cultures.

Four main challenges are developed to engage children as scientists, museum curators, and reporters. These are presented in the following diagram.

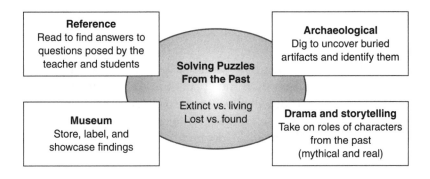

The following centers might be set up in the classroom to support the children's work.

Reading reference center	Children research from books the questions they have posed: Which was the first dinosaur? What is the largest dinosaur? Are all dinosaurs meat eaters? How did dinosaurs die?
Archaeological digs: Sand center Outside garden	Replicas of artifacts are hidden in the sand, an area that has been marked off with strings to form a grid. The task of the children is to dig up the artifacts, record them on grid paper as drawings, and to identify what they are and where they are from using the reference materials in the classroom.
Math	Lengths of tape are fixed to the hallway floor. Students have to determine how they will measure the lengths of dinosaurs and how they will find out what dinosaurs are there.
Museum	Children are involved in the labeling, categorizing, and recording through drawings and descriptions of the artifacts they discover.
Storytelling/role plays	They tell and dramatize adventures of paleontologists and archaeologists and have tales of pirates or pyramids to read from. Their stories would be recorded and children would have an opportunity to act them out.
Culminating activity: sharing our learning with home	Parents are invited to the classroom to visit the site and the museum. Children develop rules for the visit and take parents on tours through the museum and the dig site.

A question principals may want to ask is the following: Are we providing our children with the opportunities to be mentored in the thinking skills that will allow them to consider problems from various perspectives as scientists, architects, archivists, reporters, journalists, lawyers, medical doctors, technicians, mechanics, and environmentalists?

Extending Our Understanding to Other Dispositions and Disciplines

The previous example relates to a disposition of inquiry and the discipline of science. There is much more. Each disposition has a particular way of thinking, a particular literacy, and particular terms of reference (words, phrases) that shape the way we think about particular kinds of problems. In order to lay a solid foundation, children not only need to be exposed to different ways of thinking about problems, but they also need opportunities to take on this thinking through role play.

Materials should be reflective of the different dispositions we are hoping to foster in our youngest learners. So for the disposition of design, materials should allow children to manipulate shape, texture, size, measurement, and color.

There are many other possibilities using the integrated framework of the dispositions. Some of them are listed here for consideration:

- Art gallery
- Restaurant
- Mechanic shop
- Grocery store
- TV studio
- Court room
- Conservation area
- Recycle depot
- Architecture office

TIMETABLES

Samples of timetables are provided for principals so that they can develop structures that support young children's learning and guide teachers in the best ways to use instructional time.

In successful literacy classrooms, longer time is taken for assignments and less emphasis is placed on filling the day with multiple and shorter tasks. The focus of the classroom is on sustained study over time. One example of how this might be accomplished is provided in the following timetables for half- and full-day programs:

Half Day

Time	Activity
10 minutes	Arrival: Children sign in (individual writing), organize materials brought from home, select centers on planning board, and then self-select from available books (individual and shared reading).
15 minutes	Morning meeting: Attention grabber: introduction to new resources, activities, challenges for the day (modeled writing).
60+ minutes	Projects/interest centers: Children work at selected centers (individual writing, shared writing).
15 minutes	Cleanup: Children return materials into bins and storage units according to their labels (words and drawn symbols).
20 minutes	Morning circle: Review of morning's work with children (representations), sharing of stories (dramatizations) and books (read aloud).
45 minutes	Physical activity: Outdoor and indoor movement, activity, play, walks.
	Lunch

Full Day

Time	Activity
10 minutes	Arrival: Children sign in (individual writing), organize materials brought from home, select centers on planning board, and then self-select from available books (individual and shared reading).
15 minutes	Morning meeting: Attention grabber: introduction to new resources, activities, challenges for the day (modeled writing).
60+ minutes	Projects/interest centers: Children work at selected centers (individual writing, shared writing).
15 minutes	Cleanup: Children return materials into bins and storage units according to their labels (words and drawn symbols).

Time	Activity
15 minutes	Morning circle: Review of morning's work with children (representations), sharing of stories (dramatizations) and books (read aloud).
45 minutes	Physical activity: Outdoor and indoor movement, activity, play, garden, outdoor investigations, walks.
	Lunch
10 minutes	Arrival: Children sign in (individual writing), organize materials brought from home, select centers on planning board, and then self-select from available books (individual and shared reading).
15 minutes	Afternoon meeting: Attention grabber: introduction to new resources, activities, challenges for the day (modeled writing).
60+ minutes	Visits to the library/trips to local sites/businesses/participation in apprenticeship activities with a local expert (extension of the project work and interest centers).
15 minutes	Experiential response: Children respond to the experience through art, drama, building, recording.
15 minutes	Afternoon circle: Review of afternoon's work with children (representations), sharing of stories (dramatizations) and books (read aloud).
45 minutes	Physical activity: Outdoor and indoor movement, activity, play, garden, outdoor investigations, walks.

COMMUNICATION WITH PARENTS

The principal has a role to play in establishing the protocols for how and when teachers communicate with parents.

Too often, communication between home and school turns into a blame game. Our common purpose in the early years is to support and nurture the development of young children and their learning. The goal of communication with parents has to be to build bridges between home and school and to form partnerships between the parent and teachers early and develop relationships that will last throughout their elementary school years.

There are multiple methods of communication that include notes, phone calls, and face-to-face contacts. Early years teachers are adaptive in the use of these resources and open to exploring alternate avenues. When parents lack proficiency in written or verbal language, teachers provide opportunities for parents to see what is going on by inviting them in to participate more directly in classroom activities. For families with greater needs and fewer resources, the teacher increases contact with the home.

The following communication methods can be used effectively to involve parents:

- Introductory letter to parents
- Phone calls
- Newsletters
- Communication books
- Conferences with parents
- Home visits
- Class visits
- Invitation to culminating celebrations
- Presentation and discussion of children's work/portfolios
- Video recording viewing of children working
- Make-and-take sessions for home
- Borrow-a-book programs and shared reading programs
- Parent volunteer programs
- Parent workshops for reading aloud and shared reading

CHAPTER SUMMARY

This chapter provides the tools that instruction leaders will require to lead the charge toward developing a more comprehensive and inclusive early literacy program. Each of these tools has been replicated at the end of the book in the "Tools for School Leaders" section for ease of access.

Principals are encouraged to develop a vision by performing a gap analysis, developing common beliefs and guiding principles with teams, to define key literacy expectations, to review assessment strategies, to walk through classrooms looking for particular evidence, to revise and reconceptualize traditional unit plans, to develop conducive timetables, and to communicate frequently with parents regarding children's learning. For each of these questions, leaders will want to collect evidence to support their conclusions.

QUESTIONS FOR DISCUSSION

- What inspires us as a staff?
- What outcomes do we hope to achieve with our students?
- Where are we now (with respect to curriculum design, instruction, goals, assessment practices, and discipline)?
- What are the principles that guide our work?
- Do our literacy expectations balance social-emotional development, intellectual development, and the acquisition of meaningful and useful skills?
- Do our assessment practices help us understand the way children are constructing their knowledge and understanding and to monitor these over time?
- Does our literacy program demonstrate more or less of the criteria for a supportive environment, timetables, units of study, projects, resources and materials, teaching strategies, media representation, circles and meetings, assessment, and language and literacy development?
- Are we offering a balanced literacy program?
- Do the topics of study chosen have the potential for "great" literacy learning and are they topics worth studying?
- What type of challenges do we use to engage young children in their learning?
- What projects have arisen out of students' interests?
- What models do we use to structure our planning? How do story, multiple intelligences, and dispositions for learning factor into our learning?
- Are there units of study that we can reconceptualize to integrate some of these features?
- Do the timetables we have developed support sustained study over time?
- What communication strategies do we use to involve parents in the learning of their children?

CHAPTER 4

Continuous Improvement

Next Steps

Once the groundwork for improvement is in place, how does the school leader keep the momentum of improvement going? This chapter responds to this big question and provides practical strategies for principals for sustaining professional teaching teams and professional learning conversations, and for setting goals and making decisions using evidence from the classroom.

CREATING PROFESSIONAL LEARNING CONVERSATIONS

Embedded within the school organization, there has to be the means for teams of teachers to meet on a regular basis to discuss student learning and teaching strategies. If it is not timetabled in, it is not likely to happen. Often, the principal has to be creative in finding and ensuring that this time doesn't get taken by competing priorities.

With regular time set aside and priority given for professional conversations in the early years, much of the discussion among teachers should revolve around the documented evidence of student learning and the next steps for extending and expanding student thinking. Teachers can discuss how they will weave reading and writing into their plans and how they will adapt plans to match the interests of the students in their classes. Teachers should also spend a fair amount of time on understanding the child's thinking. The process outlined below is a good way for principals to get conversations going, introduce anecdotal evidence, raise assumptions, and elucidate the teacher's and children's thinking.

Teachers Examining Their Practice Through Anecdotes From the Classroom

While it is uncommon to hear teachers of young children discussing theories of practice, it is common to hear teachers telling stories of their experiences in the classroom.

For school leaders and staff developers, stories told by teachers of their classroom experiences can be a medium for understanding the nature of early years classrooms and the roles of the teacher and child in that context, as well as the pedagogical dilemmas presented there. Stories can be used as evidence to be analyzed and shared with colleagues to further understanding.

In the following example, a teacher's story about journal writing illustrates how the children discover a new connection and forge new meaning. The story is used to start a conversation about how young children think, the nature of literacy, and the role the teacher plays in the development of literacy in the early years classroom.

Example: Journal Writing

At a time in their lives when children are experimenting with pictures, letters, and numbers, early years teachers provide opportunities for children to write. Children are given writing tools—paper, pencils, markers, letter stamps, traces, samples of print, and outlines to follow. Teachers organize the day so children have the opportunity to write in journals. In small groups, children sit at tables and record their ideas as drawings and pictures in notebooks designed for this purpose. The teacher moves among the children, asking questions and assisting with recording. The teacher gears responses based on the stage of their writing. For children who are drawing, the teacher asks them to describe their picture and may record the ideas they dictate as a sentence. For those interested in printing words, the teacher prints words so they can copy or sounds out words so they can print the letter sounds they identify.

A teacher we will call Brenda tells the story of an experience that occurred during journal writing in her first year of teaching four- and five-year-old children (Speir, 1995).

> *Two girls were actively engaged in writing their journals in my classroom. I encourage my students to share their ideas so I was not surprised to see them looking back and forth at each other's work. One asked the question, "What did you write?"*
>
> *The other answered, "It's my dad's name." The first child was quick to respond that she had written her dad's name too. After comparing pages again, they were excited to discover that their dad's names were the same. Eager to share this discovery with me, they ran over and said, "Mrs. MacDonald, look! Our dads have the same name."*
>
> *I looked at their journals and sure enough the names were identical: DAD.*

Teaching teams or groups of early years teachers might be brought together to share their stories. At the first meeting, they share their stories. They might agree to discuss them then or to write responses to the stories and then come together at a later time to discuss the responses. The different responses elicit common themes and meanings that serve to get the conversation going.

When asked what the story means to her, Brenda, the teacher, crafts the following written response.

> *We have come to this classroom from different places and different situations.*
>
> *I am small with dark hair and brown eyes,*
>
> *You are tall with blond hair and blue eyes.*

I am four,

You are six.

I have lived here all my life,

You have moved from another city.

My parents are married,

Yours are divorced.

I have a temper,

You are so easy-going.

And yet our eyes sparkle with glee and our voices are filled with excitement when we find a way in which we connect.

When teachers examine and discuss their stories, they can look at several features of the story:

- Central theme(s)
- Teacher's role
- Children's role
- Qualities of the children's thinking
- Lessons learned

In this example, for the teacher, the most apparent theme in this story is the connection the children develop over the discovery that their dads have the same name. In discussion, she talks about how these children maintained this connection for about two weeks, doing everything together. She concludes that the physical differences, including age, appearance, and family background, don't matter; the experience shared is what brings people together. When she considers the randomness of this association made on this particular day, she wonders how many experiences like this go on daily in the classroom beyond the awareness of the teacher. She comments that this experience would not have been as important to her if she had not been there to observe the process and overhear the children talking.

- Central theme—connection through learning
- Teacher's role—observer
- Children's role—interpreting experience
- Qualities of the children's thinking—Dad is my dad's name, learning is shared, and the emotional qualities sustained over time
- Lessons learned—teacher does not always see children's learning; observer is a valid role for furthering understanding; children construct their meaning from experiences; the teacher's understanding of a concept may not be the child's interpretation.

This particular story illustrates how children and adults think differently, highlighting the constructed knowledge of the child as very subjective and having affective and social qualities. Using teachers' stories as the starting point for discussion invites teachers to become researchers and recorders of children's ideas and stories, documentation that will help better understand the child. This story challenges ideas of the teacher as expert and the child as novice. In this story, the collaborative meaning that the children make of the word *Dad* is the lesson, and the children have their own interpretation of what that means.

Talking about anecdotes from the classrooms encourages teachers to be reflective, to identify and address professional problems and gain insight into what they know and what they think. It also opens the door to gathering evidence from the classroom upon which decisions can be made.

The role for principals is to provide the opportunity for these conversations to happen, to establish the frameworks for discussion, to validate the process and the evidence upon which the conversation is based, and to establish the means for providing ongoing feedback as to how the process is going and where it is leading. To be effective, professional conversations such as these require high trust among staff and school leaders.

SETTING SMART GOALS

School leaders will expect teachers to set professional goals that are SMART—specific, measurable, achievable, reasonable, and timely. The question is, how do we set goals that link to the early literacy expectations? School leaders can use the following template and the examples provided in this chapter to set goals that focus on those things that are significant.

Examples are provided for principals that build on the key learning expectations presented in Chapter 3. They emphasize comprehension, meaning making, and thinking strategies rather than pure application of isolated skills. The measures for these goals include soft evidence that comes from teacher observation, anecdotal evidence, and classroom artifacts.

School leaders can encourage teachers of young children to use their collections (portfolios and projects) for this purpose. Examining these records and looking for the qualities of higher level thinking, comprehension, and understanding of meaning tell us more about where a young child is in his or her thinking than records of how many sounds he or she can produce given a page of alphabet letters.

For each goal, an indicator of success, measure, and target is developed. Principals can use these examples to promote worthy goals and frame the collection of evidence in important ways.

Smart Goal Template

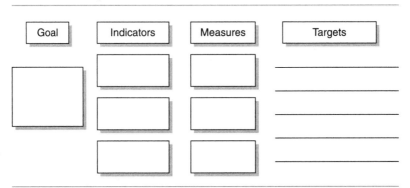

Source: Used with permission. From *The Handbook for SMART School Teams* by Anne Conzemius and Jan O'Neill. Solution Tree (formerly National Educational Service), 304 West Kirkwood Ave, Bloomington, IN 47404, 800-733-6786, www.solution-tree.com.

Examples of Early Literacy Goals

- Demonstrate comprehension of story, plot, character, and central story issues through dramatic reenactments, original stories, and dramatic works.

- Develop and use mathematical language and symbols related to quantity, size, shape, pattern, and relationships.
- Read and retell stories from books demonstrating concepts of print (left to right, front to back).
- Create expressive tones, rhythm, beat, rhyme, and sound-scapes to accompany words, poems, and speech.

Examples of Indicators of Success

- Ability to interpret story meaning and intent
- Ability to adapt ideas (stories, plots, conflicts) and to use story language in other contexts (free play, storytelling)
- Discuss qualities of shape, size, quantity, pattern, and relationships using math terms applied accurately to buildings and manipulatives
- Ability to hold the book with the top up and to move through the book from front to back, tracking print from left to right, and so forth
- Select and produce expressive means to voice meaning of words, poems, and speech

Examples of Measures

- Dramatic reenactments, scribed stories, video recordings of play using props
- Teacher's anecdotal notes, scribed descriptions, student-made diagrams of buildings and structures
- Buddy-reading records, running records, concept of print assessments, video recordings of children reading
- Audio recordings of choral readings, video recordings of chants and rhymes

Examples of Targets

- In June of the first year of kindergarten, 85% of students will retell fairy tales and myths that have been read in class through dramatic portrayals of the character and central story issues.
- In March, 90% of second-year students will recognize and use language to describe mathematical relationships and to solve mathematical problems.
- By December of the first year of kindergarten, 100% will be able to retell simple pattern stories using picture clues, track print, and pick out words and letters.

- In June of the second year of kindergarten, 75% of students will be able to create sound experiences to accompany signs, quotes, and poetry reading.

EVIDENCE-BASED DECISION MAKING

After teachers have set goals and targets, they will develop criteria for assessing student work. School leaders and teachers of young children use the idea of assessment of learning based on continuums of learning from novice, apprentice, master, and expert. They develop descriptors and examples for each of the stages in relation to the key learning expectations of early literacy. Collaborating with teachers who teach younger and older children will assist in developing age-appropriate expectations. Showing children samples of work above their level and having them work with others slightly above their level increases student awareness, helps them set achievable goals, and assists them in taking the next step in their own development of skills. Knowing where students are on this continuum is helpful for grouping children in working pairs on particular tasks. Educators must be open to revamping these continuums, for as teachers become more skilled in teaching young children, they will find that the standards achieved in the first few years may become the beginner level for children who have been exposed to the more enriched teaching that should evolve with experience. Note: This template can be found in the "Tools for School Leaders" on page 135 (Tool 11).

Assessing Student Work

	Novice "Beginner"	Apprentice "Practicing"	Master "Performing"	Expert "Teaching Others"
Recall/Retell				
Comprehension				
Conventions				
Organization				
Problem Solving				
Communication				
Application				

The term *evidence* is used rather than *data*, as the basis for decision making, because it is more inclusive in nature, including both hard statistics and soft artifacts so readily available in the classroom and school. A combination of the two is necessary to develop a more complete comprehension of what is.

When principals are assessing teacher performance, the same thing applies. Classroom evidence, including teacher notes, student work, videos of teaching practice, parent communication, and reports to parents, is as relevant and perhaps more meaningful than final evaluations or scores.

The work that teachers produce as a result of their professional conversations, the goals, and their decision making based on evidence are rich sources of evidence for appraising teacher performance and professional growth.

TEACHER PROFESSIONAL DEVELOPMENT

Teachers' professional development and professional goals can be approached in a number of ways. One way is to review the "look-fors" outlined in Chapter 3 and to determine with teachers the gaps between "where we are now" and "where we would like to be" by selecting from the checklist areas for improvement and professional development.

In *The Handbook for SMART School Teams*, Conzemius and O'Neill (2002) suggest that once teachers have set SMART goals, they can use a similar template to develop professional development goals that will assist them in meeting the targets for student achievement. This is a good process, since it makes teachers accountable for the application of their own professional development. The more closely tied the professional development plan is to teachers' classroom SMART goals, the more effective they are likely to be.

Principals should be prepared to support teachers in their professional plan, whether through access to time, finance, personnel, or materials.

Finally, when principals are conducting performance reviews, teachers should be given the opportunity to display evidence of success using portfolios and children's work from their classrooms.

CHAPTER SUMMARY

In this final chapter, the elements required for ongoing school improvement in the area of early literacy are provided: strategies for sustaining professional learning conversations, developing SMART goals that align with early literacy expectations, using children's work as the foundation for decision making about children's next learning steps, and developing professional development plans that align with all of the above.

QUESTIONS FOR DISCUSSION

- What is the focus of our professional conversations?
- What goals have we set? Are these goals SMART?
- What are the criteria we use to assess student work?
- What gaps do we perceive in our practice?
- What is the focus of our professional development?

Conclusion

As in the story of *Old Turtle and the Broken Truth*, as school leaders, we quest like the young protagonist, to find the whole truth, having been exposed only to the broken truth. Like the wise old turtle, this book acts as the guide to help find the way. The turtle taught that there are many small truths and that when we are prepared to hear, we will understand that together the small truths make up the whole truth.

The purpose of this book is to provide school leaders with a synopsis of the topic of early literacy and an understanding of how to use the potential of the early years to make a difference in literacy learning over the long term.

In conclusion, there are key messages that principals should take away from this reading. First and foremost, we have to open our minds and hearts to learn the truth from our youngest children, who are in the process of constructing their own understandings. We know that literacy learning in the early years lays the foundation for later literacy learning. Rather than reducing Grade 1 curriculum to simplified versions, school teams should be developing richer experiences for children that promote broader and deeper literacy understandings, especially for those children who come to school with limited home literacy experiences, for in a competitive global world, what counts in literacy is not how well or how much you read, but how deeply you think about what you have read.

Principals have a key role to play in the development of programs that support our youngest learners in schools. They must be aware that young children learn differently from older children, so the methods used in early years and in kindergarten will be different. They recognize that language (words, meanings, ideas, and symbols) develops out of social discourse and intellectual play. They support the creation of rich and complex learning environments that feed the young child's need to dramatize stories, tell tall tales, manipulate media, and interact with peers who are the same age, older, and younger. Principals understand that children are in the process of constructing knowledge from problem finding and problem solving about the world around them, so they provide the very best they can in authentic materials for them to work with, while actively resisting the use of workbooks and dittos.

The principal's role is to bring to the surface the erroneous beliefs and assumptions, primarily among teachers but also secondarily with parents, and to build common understandings and guiding principles that honor and recognize the potential of the young child. School leaders recognize that teachers' perceptions make a big difference in how successful young children will be in school. School leaders must help teachers understand how their beliefs shape their expectations and convey messages to children about their ability to learn. By focusing on developing exemplary practices through the use of time, texts, teaching, talk, tasks, and testing, the school leader carves out excellent early literacy programs. By building literacy partnerships in the school and outside of the school, the principal creates an inclusive literacy community, ensuring that young children have the time and support to practice their emerging skills with older and younger aged peers. The school leader works with teaching teams toward more flexible practices and constructivist approaches, where the teacher as a co-investigator and partner-in-learning, asks questions about children's learning, and collects evidence and interprets this evidence in order to make decisions and plans. The school leader recognizes the multifaceted components of planning required for success that include designing the learning environment, providing for same age and different age peer interactions, documenting children's thinking, and building partnerships with peers.

The school leader develops and sustains a vision of early literacy with the school's teaching teams, leads teams in the development of guiding principles for early literacy programs, establishes the key learning expectations with staff, and makes explicit what will be used as evidence of learning. The school leader is visible in classrooms. By walking around the school, the school leader observes children's learning and develops an awareness of where the school is and what areas to focus on for professional development. A list of what to look for has been provided in Chapter 3 (Tool 4) to get principals started.

As an instructional leader, the principal assists teachers in taking their planning to new and deeper levels by working through different planning strategies. A series of frameworks allows principals to work with teachers from the simple to the more complex in their planning, allowing them to develop deeper understandings and provide deep learning for young children. The process of reconceptualizing traditional unit plans is a powerful means for teachers to understand the differences in these planning schemes and to get them into the habit of reflecting on their practices and on continual improvement. Samples of timetables and communication strategies with parents give principals ideas about how they can support teachers and how they can gain parent support for early literacy programs.

Finally, the school leader has to build a plan for continuous improvement in order to sustain the changes made and to ensure ongoing enhancements. The components required to build professional learning communities include teachers sharing and examining stories from the classroom, setting SMART goals, and using evidence for decision making. When the principal provides concrete examples and models for teachers of what this looks like, they begin to share the vision, understand what needs to be done, and readily adapt practices.

Developing successful early literacy programs requires school leaders who develop shared visions and the courage to make long-term differences for young children. Learn from the best . . . and learn from the children . . . their future depends on it!

And just as in the story *Old Turtle and the Broken Truth,* when educators begin to see the fit . . . "some will frown, some will smile, some will even laugh and some may cry . . . eventually they will begin to understand."

Tools for School Leaders

TOOL 1: CHECKLIST FOR A LITERATE RICH ENVIRONMENT

- Emphasizes open-ended responses to a variety of experiences
- Includes environmental signs and labels displayed at the eye level of children for functional purposes (open, closed, children's names)
- Includes sign-in and sign-up sheets
- Includes white boards with markers and magnetic letters and words
- Provides many good quality books, audiobooks, reference books, handmade books, children's scribed stories, books in all areas of the room
- Provides books, stories, and songs that reflect children's experience and the experience of others (including culture and ethnicity)
- Encourages daily stories, books as starting points, books as references
- Includes chart stories
- Includes recorded questions
- Provides paper and pencils in all areas of the room
- Provides aesthetic media (scarves, streamers, musical instruments, paint, clay, art materials, and dramatic play props)

TOOL 2: CHECKLIST FOR ASSESSING THE GAPS IN LITERACY PROGRAMS

	Then	*Now*	*Ahead*
Curriculum Design	❏ TAUGHT curriculum ❏ Teacher INSTRUCTION ❏ Teacher as expert ❏ Whole group instruction ❏ Teacher-designed activities	❏ LEARNED curriculum ❏ Teacher INSTRUCTION with teacher-designed activities ❏ Child as learner ❏ Whole and small group lessons ❏ Some student choices	❏ NEGOTIATED curriculum ❏ Student CONSTRUCTION of knowledge in collaboration with teacher ❏ Child and teacher as learners ❏ Individual and group contributions to projects and investigations
Instruction	❏ Teacher dominates ❏ Whole group instruction ❏ Teacher-designed activities	❏ Whole and small group lessons organized by the teacher ❏ Some student choices in teacher-designed activities	❏ Individual and group contributions to lessons and ongoing projects and investigations
Goals	❏ Socialization goals ❏ Reading as a goal	❏ Literacy and numeracy goals (phonemes, reading strategies)	❏ Integrated understandings of literacy (across the curriculum)
Assessment	❏ Teacher as assessor ❏ Local curriculum	❏ Standard curriculum ❏ External standards	❏ Collaborative and self-assessment on continuums of learning (standards based)
Discipline	❏ Discipline by fear	❏ Discipline by choice	❏ Discipline by design

TOOL 3: KEY LITERACY EXPECTATIONS

(a) Social-Emotional/Affective Development

- Learn social conventions (taking turns, tone of voice, eye contact, acknowledging another's ideas)
- Recognize and develop empathy related to feelings and mood
- Learn moral and ethical lessons
- Take on various roles (develop perspective, make personal connections)
- Develop an awareness of cultural similarities and differences

(b) Intellectual Development

- Make sense of experience, seeking explanations
- Theorize about cause and effect
- Make predictions
- Hypothesize about observations
- Analyze and synthesize information
- Develop personal connections and express feeling responses

(c) Development of Useful and Meaningful Skills

Linguistic

- Tell, dictate, and dramatize personal, cultural, and invented stories
- Read and retell stories from books, demonstrating concepts of print (left to right, front to back)
- Understand symbols and begin to make connections between sounds and symbols, symbols and meanings (letter names and sounds, phonemes, rhyme, letter recognition and formation, word families, invented spellings)
- Experiment with words, word sounds, word order, and meanings, incorporating new vocabulary, meanings, and rules of speech
- Show that words are units of meaning (read and write names, environmental signs)
- Experiment with expression and representation of ideas and feelings using movement, dance, talk, writing, drawing, story forms, paint, music, dramatic play, symbols (numbers, gestures, pictures), and so forth
- Listen and interpret play, talk, pictures, story, symbol, and print
- Ask questions about facts, the physical world, and relationships
- Observe real-life settings where reading and writing are used

(Continued)

(Continued)

Logical-Mathematical

- Develop and use mathematical language and symbols related to quantity, size, shape, pattern, and relationships
- Use specific language to explain procedures
- Sort, classify and order, name, and describe the categories and relationships
- Identify problems and use strategies for solving problems (asking questions, posing problems, collecting and recording information, identifying patterns, determining outcomes)
- Use senses to observe and make discoveries
- Predict events based on observations

Spatial/Visual

- Use media (rigid and fluid) to communicate stories, ideas, and experiences
- Develop a visual vocabulary related to line, texture, color, shape, space, and pattern
- Make personal connections to works of art (including art, music, live performance, dance, film, and video) and develop personal responses
- Demonstrate an understanding of visual media as a language (predict next action, illustrate stories)

Musical/Rhythmic

- Develop and use music vocabulary related to beat, tone, and so forth
- Respond to music through movement, art, poetry, and sound
- Create rhythm, beat, rhyme, and soundscapes

Bodily-Kinesthetic

- Develop and use vocabulary related to movement
- Manipulate tools and instruments with purpose and control
- Express ideas, issues, and emotions through dance/movement
- Recall and re-create using materials (dramatic play)

Interpersonal and Intrapersonal

- Communicate feelings and ideas
- Act as a member of a community, negotiating, sharing, and caring
- Explore new roles: imaginings, feelings, and attitudes

TOOL 4: CHECKLIST FOR WALK-THROUGHS

	A Good Early Literacy Program IS	A Good Early Literacy Program IS NOT
Classroom Environment	❏ Language-rich environment (talk, talk, talk, print, print, print in context) ❏ Student engagement ❏ Student questions	❏ Dittos ❏ Teacher-directed circles (30 minutes) ❏ Teacher talk dominates
Timetables	❏ Large blocks of time for self-directed activity/play	❏ Short activity sessions and large blocks of time for instruction
Units of Study	❏ Meaningful topics of study ❏ Designed around BIG ideas large enough for diversity of ideas and inclusion ❏ Negotiated between children's ideas/interests and teacher's knowledge of children's interests ❏ Story-based units of study based on binary opposites ❏ Focused on the dispositions of learning ❏ Authentic links to the natural and real world ❏ Apprenticeships	❏ Small ideas of little consequence (story character such as *Clifford the Big Red Dog*, the color red)
Projects	❏ Emerge from children's ideas and interests: shadows, puddles, tall buildings, construction sites, nature, etc.	❏ Decided and designed by the teacher ❏ Narrow focus ❏ Single outcomes ❏ Little choice for students

(Continued)

(Continued)

	A Good Early Literacy Program IS	A Good Early Literacy Program IS NOT
	❏ Develop over time. Sufficient time is dedicated to the project to allow discussion of new ideas, negotiation, conflicts, revisiting ideas, note progress, and to see movement of ideas ❏ Concrete, personal from real experiences, important to children, should be large enough for diversity of ideas ❏ Rich in interpretive and representational expression ❏ Multiple means of representing and communicating meaning ❏ Stimulates activity and discussion	❏ Paper-pencil focus ❏ Little meaning ❏ Engages only a few "good" children ❏ Quiet
Resources and Materials	❏ Rich materials designed to elicit the languages of science, social studies, music, dance, drama, and mathematics ❏ Rich in interpretive and representational expression ❏ Media include paint, modeling clay, rich texture materials, building and construction materials (tiles, wood, blocks), dramatic materials (scarves, baskets, streamers), science materials (sand, water) ❏ Manipulatives such as things that pour, float, etc.	❏ Dittos, flashcards ❏ One-dimensional materials (number cards) ❏ One- and two-dimensional qualities ❏ Limited potential and appeal for children ❏ Traditional teaching materials (letters and numbers)

	A *Good Early Literacy Program* IS	A *Good Early Literacy Program* IS NOT
Teaching Strategies	❑ Teachers prepare the environment for active exploration and interaction ❑ Teachers work alongside children to facilitate their involvement by asking questions, offering suggestions, adding more complex materials or ideas to a situation ❑ Teachers accept children's ideas and use them in their planning ❑ Teachers scaffold ideas of the children	❑ Teacher directed and teacher designed ❑ Teacher talk dominates ❑ Irrelevant to children and their interests
Media Representation	❑ Multiple, creative, constructive ❑ Opportunities for exploration: What is this material? What does it do? What can I do with the material? ❑ Variation in color, texture, pattern: help children see the colors, tones, hues; help children feel the texture, the similarities and differences ❑ Presented in an artistic manner, it too should be aesthetically pleasing to look at it, should invite you to touch, admire, inspire ❑ Revisited throughout many projects to help children see the possibilities	❑ One- and two-dimensional ❑ Single purposed ❑ Primary colors ❑ Only used at particular times and for particular reasons ❑ Teacher directed

(Continued)

(Continued)

	A Good Early Literacy Program IS	A Good Early Literacy Program IS NOT
Circles and Meetings	❑ Short meetings of 10 minutes ❑ Small group, guided and shared reading ❑ Small group games	❑ Longer than 10–15 minutes ❑ Children are expected to sit, watch, be quiet, listen ❑ Teacher dominates, talking to the whole group, and telling children what to do ❑ Teacher questions focus on low-level thinking
Assessment	❑ Teachers record children's learning and progress through visual representations of their ideas ❑ Photos, anecdotal descriptions, children's work, video and audio recordings, performances, events, projects, questions, experiments, three-dimensional structures	❑ Single-page tests ❑ Focused on letters, sounds, numbers
Language and Literacy Development	❑ Opportunities to see how reading and writing are useful, modeled by people who use these skills to communicate	❑ Isolated skills such as single letters, reciting the alphabet, singing the ABC song, letter sounds, coloring, forming letters and numbers

	A Good Early Literacy Program IS	A Good Early Literacy Program IS NOT
	❏ Authentic and meaningful experiences with language and literacy: listening to and reading stories and poems; taking field trips; dictating ideas, stories, and signs; seeing print in use; participating in dramatic play and other experiences requiring communication; talking informally with people; experimenting with writing by drawing, copying, and inventing their own spelling	

TOOL 5: CHECKLIST FOR ASSESSING THE COMPONENTS OF BALANCED LITERACY

Meetings and Circle Times

- Brief and to the point (10 minutes)
- Meet in small groups, ideally five children
- Initiate thinking and activity through challenges, materials, and so forth
- Review and reflect and share children's work and ideas

Read-Alouds: Daily and Frequent

- During circle times, to prompt children's thinking
- Following project times to sum up, to advance children's thinking
- During project times (with an individual or small group), from a self-selected book to address a child's or children's question (read by a volunteer specific to an area such as the classroom library)
- During sharing/reflection time, from a child's dictation for dramatization or to share an investigation

Shared Reading

- At arrival, children self-select books and read them in pairs, small groups, or on their own.
- During project times, books and print material are available for children to read together in small groups to advance their thinking and answer their questions.
- During sharing/reflection time, teachers and children read from dictated text.

Individual Reading

- At arrival, children self-select books and read them in pairs, small groups, or on their own.
- Read-aloud books stay in the classroom library for children to read on their own.
- Children read signs and organize materials according to signs and labels.

Modeled Writing

- Teachers record children's dictation.
- Teachers create environmental signs conveying messages for children to decode (closed, open, exit, entrance, stop, go) and sign-up sheets for centers, projects, turns, and so forth.

Shared Writing

- Children create their own messages with the teachers' help.

Individual Writing

- Children sign in each morning (record name on a chart).
- Children sign in to interest centers.
- Representational writing including recorded math work, for example, patterns by one, two, or three dimensions.

TOOL 6: CHECKLIST FOR ASSESSING LITERACY PROJECTS

Criteria for a Good Project

- A project emerges from children's ideas and interests
- The teacher knows the interest to children (e.g., can introduce a project: shadows, puddles, tall buildings, construction sites, nature, etc.)
- A project is long enough to develop over time, to incorporate new ideas, to allow negotiation, to provoke conflict of ideas, so that ideas can be revisited, and so that progress of ideas is evident
- A project is often concrete, comes from real experiences, is important to children, is broad enough to allow for a diversity of ideas and rich in its potential for interpretive/representational expression

Steps in Developing a Project
Teacher planning:

- Brainstorm and create a web of ideas from a topic.
- Outline important events.
- Look into sites, sources, and experts to further the study and put it into a real world context.
- Collect resources.

Step 1: Planning With Students

- Stimulate the children's interest in the topic through a story, video, or object.
- Collect ideas and map out what children already know.
- List questions children would like to investigate/answer.

Step 2: Project Work

- Discuss and record what questions they have, whom they might talk to, and what they might bring to the classroom. Discuss what they are likely to see and do.
- On trips, take field notes and make sketches and decide what they would like to learn more about.
- People with firsthand experience of the topics through their work or travel may come to visit and talk with children, respond to questions, and engage in discussion.
- Discuss trips; re-create accounts of what happened, whom they talked with, what they saw, and what they learned. Sketches can become the basis for drawings, paintings, and construction of models; information books are consulted; new questions are raised and letters written. Plan follow-up activities.

Step 3: Culminating Event/Celebration of Learning

- Showcase the children's work to other children, parents, and staff through a display, a performance, or an event.
- Children personalize the new knowledge by presenting it through imaginative stories and dramatic sequences.

Adapted from Sylvia Chard's (2001) work on *The Project Approach in Early Childhood and Elementary Education*. For more examples, visit www.projectapproach.org.

TOOL 7: PLANNING TEMPLATE USING A MYTHIC FRAMEWORK

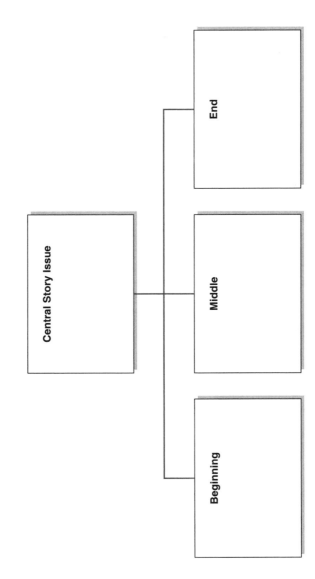

TOOL 8: PLANNING TEMPLATE USING THE MULTIPLE INTELLIGENCES

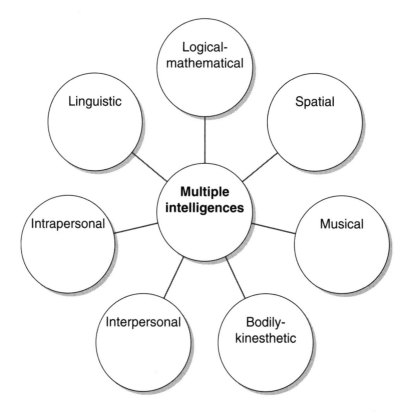

TOOL 9: INTEGRATED PLANNING FRAMEWORK CHART

Discipline	Habits of Mind or Dispositions	Roles Children Take On	Literacy
Science	Inquiry model: Asking questions, developing hypothesis, collecting information, analyzing data, drawing conclusions	Archaeologist Paleontologist Doctor Scientist Computer Investigator Detective Police Officer	Experiments, lab reports, diagrams
History/social studies	Recording and documenting events: dating, labeling, storing	Archivist Curator Historian Museum	Timelines, stories, historical records, plays, artifacts
Mathematics	Measuring and quantifying, classifying and sorting, finding patterns, understanding relationships, developing formulas	Accountant Statistician Architect	Graphs, tables, drawings, numbers, calculations, inventions, formulas, logic problems
Language	Communicating meaning: developing thesis, argument or idea, catching the reader's attention, developing plausibility, stringing a tale, implied meanings	Reporter Novelist Politician Speech writer Lawyer	Narratives, tall tales, reports
Art/spatial	Interpreting	Musician Artist Architect Mechanic Dancer Actor	Paintings, drawings, drafts, labels, plays

TOOL 10: PLANNING TEMPLATE USING A DISPOSITION FRAMEWORK

Disposition	Investigation	Representation

TOOL 11: TEMPLATE FOR
ASSESSING STUDENT WORK

	Novice *"Beginner"*	*Apprentice* *"Practicing"*	*Master* *"Performing"*	*Expert* *"Teaching Others"*
Recall/Retell				
Comprehension				
Conventions				
Organization				
Problem Solving				
Communication				
Application				

Must Reads

The following texts are suggested as "must reads" for school leaders.

Carreiro, P. (1998). *Tales of thinking: Multiple intelligences in the classroom.* York, ME: Stenhouse.

Chard, S. (2001). The Project Approach in early childhood and elementary education. Retrieved July 25, 2005, from www.project approach.com

Dufour, R., & Eaker, R. (1998). *Professional learning communities at work: Best practices for enhancing student achievement.* Bloomington, IN: National Educational Service.

Fraser, S. (2006). *Authentic childhood: Experiencing Reggio Emilia in the classroom* (2nd ed.). Toronto, Ontario, Canada: Thomson/Nelson.

Fullan, M. (2005). *Leadership & sustainability: System thinkers in action.* Thousand Oaks, CA: Corwin.

Jalongo, M. R., & Isenburg, J. P. (with Gerbracht, G.). (1995). *Teachers' stories: From personal narrative to professional insight.* San Francisco: Jossey-Bass.

Katz, L. (1995). *The benefits of mixed-age grouping.* Urbana, IL: ERIC Clearinghouse on Elementary and Early Childhood Education. (ERIC Document Reproduction Service No. ED382411)

Katz, L., Evangelou, D., & Hartman, J. A. (1990). *The case for mixed-age grouping in early education.* Washington, DC: National Association for the Education of Young Children.

Szarkowicz, D. L. (2006). *Observations and reflections in childhood.* Scarborough, Ontario, Canada: Nelson Thomson Learning.

Wood, D. (2003). *Old Turtle and the broken truth.* New York: Scholastic Press.

Glossary

Dispositions of learning: The habits of mind or qualities of thought required to think your way successfully through the disciplines of mathematics, science, history, technology, language, and the arts.

Documentation: Comes from work of Reggio Emilia in the form of observation and record keeping that focuses intensively on children's thinking, connections, and ideas over time often recorded as photos and scribed records of children's actions and words.

Early literacy: Characterized by opposites, metaphor, story, and the big questions in life, the thinking and the rapid language learning that occurs between the ages of three and six years is the framework for thinking and literacy learning in later years. Young children develop the dispositions that lead to proficiency in various literacy forms through play with a rich array of linguistic, logical-mathematical, spatial, bodily-kinesthetic, musical, interpersonal, intrapersonal, and naturalistic experiences.

Literacy: UNESCO's concept of literacy has moved beyond the simple notion of a set of technical skills of reading, writing, and calculating to one that encompasses multiple dimensions of these competencies. In acknowledging recent economic, political, and social transformations—including globalization and the advancement of information and communication technologies (ICTs)—UNESCO recognizes that there are many practices of literacy embedded in different cultural processes, personal circumstances, and collective structures. Literacy is central to all levels of learning, through all delivery modes. Literacy is an issue that concerns everybody. (United Nations Educational, Scientific and Cultural Organization)

Multiage: A mixed-age group or multiage group of different ages and stages that are grouped together deliberately for instructional purposes.

Projects: Collaborative real world topics. Children do field work, pursue investigations, and represent their understanding through drawing, writing, designing graphs and charts, construction, visual arts, and dramatic play. This is based on the project work of educators Katz and Chard.

Reggio Emilia approach: An educational philosophy that was developed by women in the community of Reggio Emilia, Italy, that allows children to learn from relationships with people and materials, to explore, and to express themselves in a variety of ways.

Bibliography

Allington, R. (2001). *What really matters for struggling readers: Designing research-based programs.* New York: Longman.

Allington, R. (2002). What I've learned about effective reading instruction from a decade of studying exemplary elementary classroom teachers. *Phi Delta Kappan, 83*(10), pp. 740–747.

Armstrong, T. (1994). *Multiple intelligences in the classroom.* Alexandria, VA: Association for Supervision and Curriculum Development.

Bamberger, J. (1991). The laboratory for making things: Developing multiple representations of knowledge. In D. Schön (Ed.), *The reflective turn: Case studies in and on educational practice* (pp. 37–62). New York: Teachers College Press.

Bergen, D. (2002). The role of pretend play in children's cognitive development. *Early Childhood Research and Practice, 4*(1), 2–15. Available at http://ecrp.uiuc.edu/v4n1/bergen.html

Bloom, B. (1981). *All our children learning.* New York: McGraw-Hill.

Bransford, J., Brown, A., & Cocking, R. (Eds.). (2000). *How people learn: Brain, mind, experience, and school.* Washington, DC: National Academy Press.

Carnegie Task Force on Meeting the Needs of Young Children. (1994). *Starting points: Meeting the needs of our youngest children.* New York: Carnegie Corporation of New York. (ERIC Document Reproduction Service No. ED369562)

Chard, S. (2001). *The project approach in early childhood and elementary education.* Retrieved July 25, 2005, from http://www.project approach.com

Christie, J. F., & Enz, B. (1992). The effects of literacy play interventions on preschoolers' play patterns and literacy development. *Early Education and Development, 3*(3), 205–220. (ERIC Document Reproduction Service No. EJ447691)

Cogswell, D. (1996). *Chomsky for beginners.* New York: Writers & Readers.

Conzemius, A., & O'Neill, J. (2002). *The handbook for SMART school teams.* Bloomington, IN: National Educational Service.

Driscoll, M. (1994). *Psychology of learning for instruction.* Boston: Allyn & Bacon.

Dyson, A., & Genishi, C. (Eds.). (1994). *The need for story: Cultural diversity in classroom and community.* Urbana, IL: National Council of Teachers of English.

Edwards, C. P., Gandini, L., & Forman, G. E. (Eds.). (1998). *The hundred languages of children: The Reggio Emilia approach—advanced reflections* (2nd ed.). Greenwich, CT: Ablex.

Egan, K. (1997). *The educated mind: How cognitive tools shape our understanding.* Chicago: University of Chicago Press.

Einarsdottir, J. (2000). Incorporating literacy resources into the play curriculum of two Icelandic preschools. In K. A. Roskos & J. F. Christie (Eds.), *Play and literacy in early childhood: Research from multiple perspectives* (pp. 77–90). New York: Erlbaum.

Fulghum, R. (2003). *All I really need to know I learned in kindergarten: Uncommon thoughts on common things.* New York: Ballantine Books.

Fullan, M. (2005). *Leadership & sustainability: System thinkers in action.* Thousand Oaks, CA: Corwin Press.

Fyfe, B., & Forman, G. (1996). The negotiated curriculum. *Innovations in early education: The International Reggio Exchange, 3*(4), pp. 4–7.

Gardner, H. (1983). *Frames of mind: The theory of multiple intelligences.* New York: Basic Books.

Gardner, H. (1993). *Frames of mind: The theory of multiple intelligences* (with new introduction by author). New York: Basic Books.

Gardner, H., & Hatch, T. (1989). Multiple intelligences go to school: Educational implications of the theory of multiple intelligences. *Educational Researcher, 18*(8), 4–9.

Gardner, H., & Winner, E. (1979). The development of metaphoric competence: Implications for humanistic disciplines. In S. Sacks (Ed.), *On metaphor* (pp. 121–140). Chicago: University of Chicago Press.

Geddis, A., Lynch, M., & Speir, S. (1998). Bridging theory and practice: Towards a professional scholarship of pedagogy. *Teaching and Teacher Education, 14*(1), 95–106.

Kalkowski, P. (1995). *Close Up # 18: Peer and Cross-Age Tutoring. School Improvement Research Series.* Retrieved August 22, 2008, from Northwest Regional Educational Library Web site: http://www.nwrel.org/scpd/sirs/9/c018.html

Katz, L. (1993). *Dispositions, definitions and implications for early childhood practice.* Champaign, IL: ERIC Clearinghouse on Elementary and Early Childhood Education. (ERIC Document Reproduction Service No. ED360104)

Katz, L. (1995). *The benefits of mixed-age grouping.* Urbana, IL: ERIC Clearinghouse on Elementary and Early Childhood Education. (ERIC Document Reproduction Service No. ED382411)

Katz, L. (1999). *Curriculum disputes in early childhood education.* Champaign, IL: ERIC Clearinghouse on Elementary and Early Childhood Education. (ERIC Document Reproduction Service No. ED436298)

McCain, M. N., & Mustard, J. F. (1999). *Reversing the real brain drain: Early years study: Final report.* Toronto: Ontario Children's Secretariat. Available at http://www.gov.on.ca/children/graphics/stel02_183397.pdf

McCain, M. N., & Mustard, J. F. (2002). *Early years study: Three years later.* Toronto, Ontario, Canada: Founders Network.

Neuman, S. B., & Roskos, K. (1992). Literacy objects as cultural tools: Effects on children's literacy behaviors in play. *Reading Research Quarterly, 27*(3), 202–225. (ERIC Document Reproduction Service No. EJ447054)

Paley, V. G. (1981). *Wally's stories: Conversations in the kindergarten.* Cambridge, MA: Harvard University Press.

Paley, V. G. (1990). *The boy who would be a helicopter: The uses of story-telling in the classroom.* Cambridge, MA: Harvard University Press.

Paley, V. G. (1992). *You can't say you can't play.* Cambridge, MA: Harvard University Press.

Paley, V. G. (1994). Princess Annabella and the black girls. In A. H. Dyson & C. Genishi (Eds.), *The Need for Story* (pp. 145–154). Urbana, IL: National Council of Teachers of English.

Paley, V. G. (1995). *Kwanzaa and me: A teacher's story.* Cambridge, MA: Harvard University Press.

Project Zero, Harvard Graduate School of Education. (2006). *Making learning visible: Understanding, documenting, and supporting individual and group learning.* Retrieved August 22, 2008 from http://pzweb .harvard.edu/mlv/index.cfm

Putnam, L. R. (1987). Language, language development and reading (Noam Chomsky interviewed by Lillian R. Putnam), *Reading Instruction Journal, Fall 1987.* Available at http://www.chomsky .info/interviews/1987——.htm

Riddle, E., & Dabbagh, N. (1999). Lesv Vygotsky's social development theory. Retrieved August 22, 2008, from http://sfs.scnu.edu.cn/ sla/upload/2006_01/06012721308512.doc

Schütz, R. (2004). *Vygotsky & language acquisition.* Retrieved August 22, 2008, from http://www.sk.com.br/sk-vygot.html

Schweinhart, L., Barnes, H., & Weikart, D. (1993). *Significant benefits: The High/Scope Perry preschool study through age 27. Monographs of the High/Scope Educational Research Foundation, No. Ten.* Ypsilanti, MI: High/Scope Educational Research Foundation. Available at http://ceep.crc.uiuc.edu/pubs/ivpaguide/appendix/schweinhart-preschool.pdf

Schweinhart, L. J. (2003, April). *Benefits, costs, and explanations of the High/Scope Perry Preschool Program.* Paper presented at the meeting of the Society for Research in Child Development, Tampa, FL.

Shore, R. (1997). *Rethinking the brain: New insights into early development.* New York: Families and Work Institute.

Speir, S. (1995). *Stories of the classroom: Puzzles, pedagogy and practice.* Unpublished thesis dissertation, University of Western Ontario, Canada.

Speir, S. (2005, March). *In the zone: A review of peer coaching strategies in elementary school.* Paper presented at the Oxford Round Table: Emerging and Early Literacy, Oxford, England.

Stone, S. J., & Christie, J. F. (1996). Collaborative literacy learning during sociodramatic play in a multiage (K–2) primary classroom. *Journal of Research in Childhood Education, 10*(2), 123–133. (ERIC Document Reproduction Service No. EJ524973)

Szarkowicz, D. L. (2006). *Observations and reflections in childhood.* Scarborough, Ontario, Canada: Nelson Thomson Learning.

Tarr, P. (2001). *What art educators can learn from Reggio Emilia.* Retrieved August 13, 2008, from www.designshare.com/index.php/articles/aesthetic-codes-in-early-childhood-classrooms

U.S. Department of Education. (1999). *How are the children? Report on early childhood development and learning.* Retrieved August 22, 2008, from http://www.ed.gov/pubs/How_Children/index.html

Vukelich, C. (1994). Effects of play interventions on young children's reading of environmental print. *Early Childhood Research Quarterly, 9*(2), 153–170. (ERIC Document Reproduction Service No. EJ493679)

Vygotsky, L. (1962). *Thought and language.* Cambridge: MIT Press.

Vygotsky, L. (1978). *Mind in society: The development of higher psychological processes.* Cambridge, MA: Harvard University Press.

Vygotsky, L. (1986). *Thought and language* (translation newly rev. and edited by Alex Kozulin). Cambridge: MIT Press.

Weikart, D. P., Bond, J. T., & McNeil, J. T. (1978). *The Ypsilanti Perry preschool project: Preschool years and longitudinal results through fourth grade.* Ypsilanti, MI: High/Scope Educational Research Foundation.

Wood, D. (2003). *Old Turtle and the broken truth.* New York: Scholastic Press.

Yardley, A. (1988). *Exploration and language.* Oakville, Ontario, Canada: Rubicon.

Zill, N., Resnick, G., Kim, K., McKey, R. H., Clark, C., Pai-Samant, S., et al. (2001). *Head Start FACES: Longitudinal findings on program performance. Third progress report.* Washington, DC: U.S. Department of Health & Human Services. (ERIC Document Reproduction Service No. ED453969)

Index

CORWIN
PRESS

The Corwin Press logo—a raven striding across an open book—represents the union of courage and learning. Corwin Press is committed to improving education for all learners by publishing books and other professional development resources for those serving the field of PreK–12 education. By providing practical, hands-on materials, Corwin Press continues to carry out the promise of its motto: **"Helping Educators Do Their Work Better."**

ONTARIO
PRINCIPALS'
COUNCIL

The Ontario Principals' Council (OPC) is a voluntary professional association for principals and vice-principals in Ontario's public school system. We believe that exemplary leadership results in outstanding schools and improved student achievement. To this end, we foster quality leadership through world-class professional services and supports. As an ISO 9001 registered organization, we are committed to our statement that "quality leadership is our principal product."